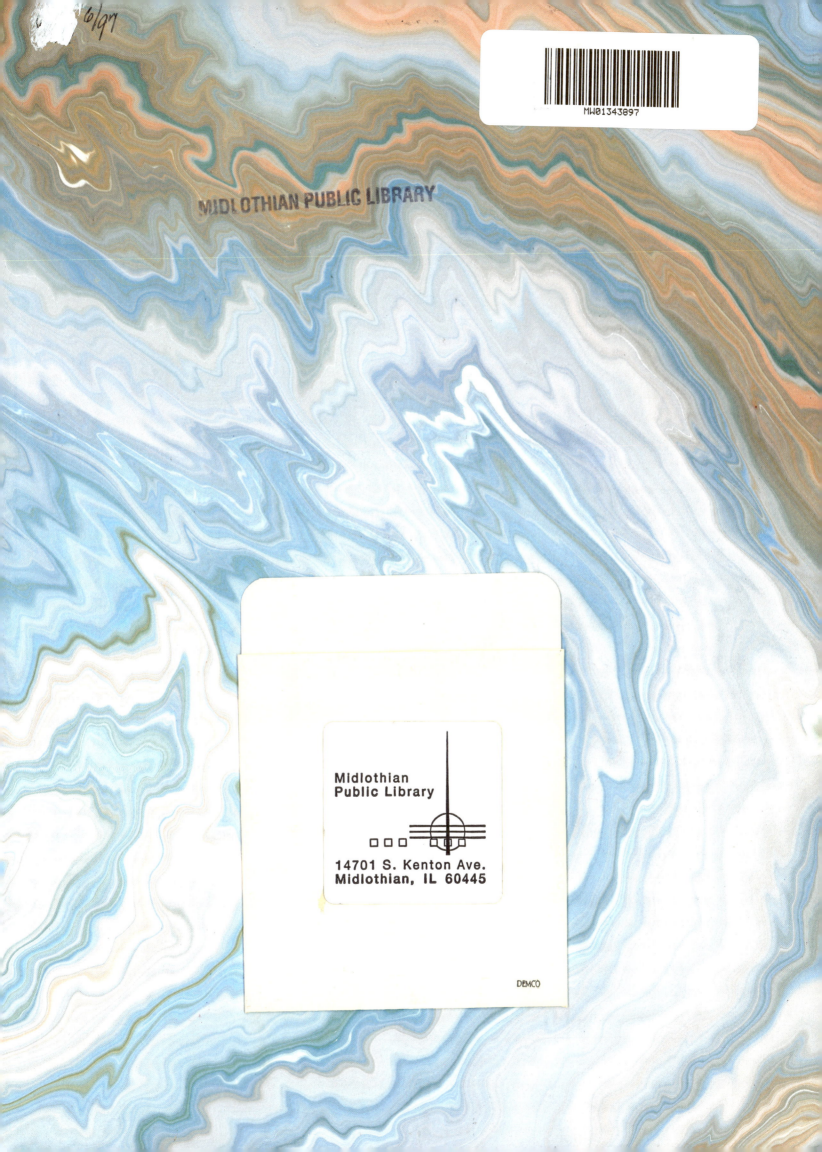

FRAGRANCE BOTTLE MASTERPIECES

Joanne Dubbs Ball and Dorothy Hehl Torem

Schiffer Publishing Ltd
77 Lower Valley Road, Atglen, PA 19310

"So many scents, so little time"!

We dedicate this book to all the fragrances
we treasured in the past,
to those special ones we now favor . . .
and, most especially,
to the bittersweet memories a chosen few
still stir within us.

Cover photograph of "Le Nu" Courtesy Lalique Parfums

Copyright © by Joanne Dubbs Ball and Dorothy Hehl Torem

All rights reserved. No part of this work may be reproduced or used in any forms or by any means--graphic, electronic, or mechanical, including photocopying or information storage and retrieval systems--without written permission from the copyright holder.

Printed in Hong Kong.
ISBN: 0-88740-985-7

Library of Congress Cataloging-in-Publication Data

Ball, Joanne Dubbs.
   Fragrance bottle masterpieces / Joanne Dubbs Ball and Dorothy Hehl Torem.
     p. cm.
   Includes bibliographical references and index.
   ISBN 0-88740-985-7 (hard)
   1. Perfume bottles--Collectors and collecting--Catalogs.
I. Torem, Dorothy Hehl. II. Title.
NK5440.B6B335 1996
748.8'2'075--dc20
                              96-17243
                               CIP

Published by Schiffer Publishing, Ltd.
77 Lower Valley Road
Atglen, PA 19310
Please write for a free catalog.
This book may be purchased from the publisher.
Please include $2.95 postage.
Try your bookstore first.

We are interested in hearing from authors
with book ideas on related subjects.

Contents

Acknowledgments 4

Preface 5

Glassmaking 6
   Ancient & European Glassmaking 7
   Glassmaking in the New World 10
      • Henry William Stiegel 13
      • John Frederick Amelung, the Gallatin Company, & the Expansion Westward 17
      • Caspar Wistar, the Stanger Brothers, the Wheaton Family, & the Legacy of South Jersey Glass 18
      • The New England Influence, From Pitkin to The New England Glass Company & Boston & Sandwich Works 20

Historical Perfumeries & Enchanted Perfumery Reproductions 23
   Chamerolles—From Medieval France, a Modern-Day Replication 24
   The Crown Perfumery 27
   Parfums Caron 30
   Elizabeth Arden Company 39

Masterpieces in Modern Glass 44
   René Lalique 45
   De Vilbiss 52
   Baccarat 53
   Saint Gobain Desjonquère 55
   Lucien Gaillard 56
   Pochet et du Courval 56
   Verreries Brosse 59
   J. Viard 59

The Bottle Beautiful ...Past & Present 60
   Non-Commercial Flacons 36
   Commercial Flacons 91
   "A Myriad of Minis" 159
   Solid Perfumes 180
   Advertising Fans 183

Factice & Display Bottles .. 191

Footnotes 249
Bibliography 250
Value Guide 251
General Index 253
Fragrance Names Index 255

Pierrot, by Les Parfums de Rosine, Paul Poiret.

ACKNOWLEDGMENTS

With very special thanks to the following, whose contributions were invaluable. We are deeply indebted to them all.

Bob Ball; Dennis Caron; Caroline Clark, representing The Crown Perfumery Company, London, and Parfums Caron, Paris; Thierry Laur, Parfums Caron, Paris; Mark B. Craig, Duggal Photo Labs, New York City; Gregg and Lin Dubbs; Susan Arnot Heany, Susan Santori, and Paul Seplowitz, Elizabeth Arden Co.; all the folks at Express Photo in Avon, Connecticut; Helen Farnsworth; Neil French; Alyson Torem-French; Ivanhoe Gadpaille; Renee Gold; Mike Gross; Arielle Hart, Mini-Scents Newsletter; Jolli/Botanica, East Greenwich, Rhode Island; Marilyn Kearney; John D. Kendig; Zion Evangelical Church, Manheim, Pennsylvania; Jane B. French and Dina Cook, Parfums Lalique, New York; Michele Matheson; James McMahon, Hershey Community Museum, Hershey, Pennsylvania; Randy Monsen, Monsen and Baer, Vienna, Virginia; Jeannie Roberts, Roberts' Antiques, Micanopy, Florida; Donna Sims, Perfume and Scent Bottle Quarterly; Gay LeCleire Taylor, Museum of American Glass, Wheaton Village, Millville, New Jersey; Jake Torem; and Sharon and Howard Weatherly.

Diorama, by Christian Dior.

PREFACE

*"The fragrance of her rich and delightful character
still lingered about the place where she had lived,
as a dried rosebud scents the drawer
where it has withered and perished."*
(Hawthorne)

Over the past centuries, thousands of beautiful and unique flacons have housed an equal number of intriguing and appealing scents. The bottles shown here are intended to also represent countless others that are equally deserving of the title "masterpiece." Throughout the long history of the perfume industry, a seemingly never-ending parade of beautiful bottles have traipsed down the "fragrance runway." Virtually all of them have attracted their share of admirers, be they modest or legion. Every outstanding bottle joins the ranks of innumerable others that have been so praised, whether by only a relative few (due to short or limited distribution) or by countless thousands. Amidst all of them, certain scents, like *Chanel No. 5*, have attained such popularity that the bottle, its contents, or both have been elevated to icon status.

The appeal of a fragrance bottle encompasses a host of preferences . . . admirers can be struck by the seemingly impossible execution of its design, the glitter of light on its multi-faceted surface, colors that glimmer like rainbows, the perfection of its engraving or enameling, or the figurals that rise proud and tall from the stopper or decorate its surface. If the word "masterpiece" passes the lips, it is most often used to express one's individual appreciation for an object that pleases the senses.

Pictured here is but a sampling of the flacons that have garnered these favored niches, not just with the sophisticated and finite community of collectors but, of equal importance, with the general public—those folks who treasure these particular bottles not only for their beauty but also for the memories they evoke, without worshiping at the shrine of their perceived value. Each bottle stands in mute testimony to the craftsmanship of many others.

Blue opaline fragrance bottle with gold enameling and engraved figurals on stopper. French, from the era of Napoleon III, it rises a stunning 8.25". Courtesy Renee Gold

GLASSMAKING

Reguete by Worth, bottle by Lalique.

It seems incongruous that a gritty substance that is a mainstay of the seashore and found in the soil is also the basic material necessary to produce glass, yet such is indeed the case. For when refined, sand—the substance of castles that woefully wash away at high tide—becomes pure silica, the raw material from which many beautiful glass objects are made.

The earliest glassmaking was accomplished in rectangular ovens. No more than simple fire pits, these ovens were efficient enough to be used for thousands of years. Indeed, "the one unearthed at Tel el Amarna in Egypt, which dates to the fourteenth century B.C., differs little from that shown in a fifteenth century painting of a Flemish glasshouse."[1] It was during this latter century, however, that the round-shaped, two-chamber oven came into use.

An American crystal glass formula from 1865 called for a mixture of materials, primarily silex, red lead, pearl ash, nitre, phosphate of lime, white oxide of antimony, manganese, arsenic, and borax. "To this refractory (hard to melt ingredient) it is necessary to add some sort of alkali which lowers the sand's melting point and makes it less brittle in its final, finished, glassy state."[2] Thus, the sparkling material called glass begins as a combination of sand and powdered chemicals, "and here only is where any secrets enter into the business of making glass."[3]

When minerals are ground into these preparations, an infinite variety of finished pieces becomes possible. For example, amber, aquamarine, and olive green shades result from ferrous and ferric iron in the sand. These are considered "natural" colors. "Artificial" ones, like pale blue, red, amethyst, orange, and yellow, require the addition of various oxides and silicates. This trial and error process, and the infinite patience of early glassmakers, has given us glorious colors and sparkling clears, all reflecting the special refraction of light that makes glass such a universally appealing product.

Another element found naturally in soil plays a related role in glassmaking: the fine clay used to make the pots in which the sand is melted and the chemicals are mixed. The delicate melting and mixing operation that takes place inside the pots must be carefully controlled so the pots do not break—spilling costly material—when their contents are melted. During the melting operation—a process that can take thirty or forty hours—the melting mixture must also be constantly monitored so impurities can be skimmed from the surface as they slowly rise to the top.

When the melting process is completed, the glassblower's magic begins. He places the pipe through the oven openings to withdraw what is termed a "gather" of molten glass, an operation that in earlier times was particularly hazardous to the glassblower's lungs. The operation from this point on is a complex one, encompassing many stages that require supreme expertise. Suffice it to say that it is a talent deserving of much admiration . . . and awe.

Whether by hand-blowing the "gather" or placing it into one of many different types of molds, glassmaking artisans from years and centuries past have left their mark on the glassmaking industry—and on the precious fragrance bottles so admired and coveted today.

Ancient & European Glassmaking

The history of glass dates back about five thousand years. "As an independent substance, glass seems to date from somewhere in the third millenium B.C. and to have been manufactured first in Mesopotamia. . . . King Tuthmosis III of Egypt invaded and began conquering Assyria in 1481 B.C., and a part of his booty is presumed to have brought back to Egypt both glass and glass workers . . ."[4] However, excavations indicate that the more complex blown glass procedures did not make an appearance until many centuries later, in the general time frame of 150 B.C.

Scents were not taken lightly, even by the ancient Egyptians. Their earliest perfume was reputed to be *Kyphi*. "Scholars have claimed that when the tomb of King Tut was opened it was this odor that issued forth. So famous was this perfume that it was later adopted by the Greeks and Romans and so was passed on to European civilizations."[5] It is important to note, however, that not until the advent of distillation processes in the seventeenth century did it become possible to enjoy liquid perfumes as we know them today. Prior to this time, scents were either solid or in the form of ointments and oils. Although the Greeks were credited with the first use of liquid perfumes, these were essentially plant-based aromatic substances that were finely ground and then suspended in oil. Many early vessels or amphoras bore resemblance to pottery ewers, urns, and vases, but were, in fact, receptacles for scented balms.

Beginning around the first century A.D. and continuing for many hundreds of years thereafter, the Roman empire was responsible for most, if not all, of the glass products dispensed to the civilized world. In fact, there is evidence of the mastery of the tube or blowpipe by Roman craftsmen shortly before the birth of Christ. When the Roman Empire later became fragmented, "the Eastern empire continued to craft; but in the West the glass houses vanished under the heels of the barbarian hoardes. A few glass blowers fled to the forests of Germany, and by the fifth century A.D. had founded the tiny shops that for the next thousand years constituted Europe's sole contribution to glassmaking history."[6] It should be noted, however, that in France, the imperial factory of Frontincennes at Forêt-Eu (founded in the second century A.D.) is purported to be the oldest in the world and is acclaimed as the seat of all Norman glassworks.

In the Middle Ages, glassmaking was revived by the Venetians, and they, along with the Crusades of the eleventh century, are credited with the expansion of the glassmaker's art into first Bohemia, France, Germany, and England, and from there throughout most of Europe. But not without some risk; "like the Romans

Ovoid scented oil jar (1390-1325 B.C.), 18th Dynasty, Memphis.

Core-formed perfume vessel (340-200 B.C.), Magna Graecia.

Scented oil perfumes (990-400 B.C.), Island of Rhodes.

Persian scent bottle (8th-9th century A.D.).

Persian scent bottle (9th-10th century A.D.)

and Byzantines before them, the Venetians took great pains to protect the secrets of the trade monopoly, even to the extent of putting to death absconding glassblowers."[7] Nonetheless, suppression was virtually impossible, and the gradual movement of Venetian artisans throughout Europe disseminated the hitherto closely-guarded details of Venetian glassmaking. One of the major secrets was the sixteenth-century discovery of adding manganese and other chemicals to the process. The result was a far less expensive glass with the clarity and purity of rock crystal. *Millifiori*, a technique employing the arrangement of threads of multi-colored glass into an exquisite vessel, was a coveted outgrowth of Venetian glassmaking skill.

As had happened elsewhere and in other times, glassmakers carried their art far and wide. During the seventh and eighth centuries, Islamic glassmaking was a flourishing industry, extending throughout the lands they conquered. The production of decorative glass featuring opaque vitreous enamels was perfected in the Near East, with the finest produced in Syria during the thirteenth and fourteenth centuries. However, once again, war and conquest played a role in the history of glassmaking. When Tamerlane attacked Damascus in 1402, many Venetian enterprises also suffered mightily in the wake of the destruction of this font of learning and industry. For some, it was a lethal blow, and the effect on the glass industry was no exception. With its craftsmen scattered and expelled, Europe was effectively isolated from the most prominent glass sources.

In the seventeenth century the English were credited with making the first leaded glass. However, "in England, glass bottles were still rather a novelty as late as the mid-seventeenth century."[8] By the eighteenth century, France was at the forefront of glassmaking techniques, being mainly credited with superiority in the mastery of medieval stained glass and engraved pieces. The French were also responsible for the nineteenth century revival of *millifiori* glass, thus contributing to many glass designs during the revolutionary Art Nouveau movement to follow. Indeed, the late nineteenth century brought with it keen interest in colored glass, which had spread from Bohemia and was enlivened in the scent bottle market by the addition of faceting and gilt. As a result of this surge in the popularity of *millifiori* and colored glass, two particular styles of scent bottles—the intricately faceted type and those

As featured in an article titled "Scent and Sensibility" (*Vogue*, April 1939), here is a grouping of seventeenth- and eighteenth-century rare miniature scent bottles on display in Elizabeth Arden's salon. The exhibition included examples from China, as well as such illustrious names as Meissen, Staffordshire, Chelsea, Furstenberg, and Créey en Valois. As the article so colorfully states,

> Certainly, in past centuries, perfume was the *grand chic* in presents. Formulas were guarded with passionate secrecy, and stored preciously in the attic in plain bottles. The essences were decanted in exquisite miniature flacons like these, when the urge to give a present arose. Such flacons of scent were, among other things, the travelling gift *de rigeur* from a gallant to his lady, intended to ease the migraine from rutted roads, dusty coaches, and lovers left behind.

Perfume flask (1st century B.C.), Eastern Mediterranean.

Bird-shaped flask for perfume (A.D. 50-200), Northern Italy.

referred to as the "frosted cameo cut"—were especially prized. Also of brilliant colorations were four- to five-inch high scent bottles fashioned with eye-catching double compartments, popular during the period around 1860.

In England, Stourbridge became an influential center for glassmaking during this era, prominently responsible for cameo scent bottles with delicate carvings decorating translucent colored glass. "The technique involved in making these vessels was long and complicated; first a translucent coloured background was blown, and then covered with an opaque layer of white glass, which was then painstakingly cut away to leave the usually floral cameo pattern."[9]

The reverse intaglio style is reputed to have been originally devised in Bohemia, with clay figures embedded in the glass, but these efforts were never perfected. However, early in the nineteenth century the Frenchman Desprez "began producing high quality portraits in a porcellanous material and by the early years of the century had succeeded in encasing them in glass."[10] Appearing almost silverlike, they evolved from mere hanging accent pieces to the central decorative focus on various bottles, including those containing fragrances.

GLASSMAKING IN THE NEW WORLD

Glassmaking on what is now American soil was virtually impossible for more than the first hundred years of colonization, and the few preliminary attempts met with little success. Early among these was a bold 1608 venture initiated by seven individuals from Holland and Poland who hoped to establish a successful glassmaking operation in Jamestown, Virginia. Although valiant, their efforts were short-lived.

As with many other complex procedures, glassmaking required not only basic business acumen but also ready and economical access to skilled workmen and raw materials. To encourage European glassmakers to venture into this virgin territory, they had to be lured with higher wages than those generally offered in their homelands. Add to this the exhorbitant taxes and restrictions levied by the British against Colonial exports, and it becomes clear why many independent ventures failed; they were over-regulated and generally under-capitalized. "The Crown was interested in selling English manufactured goods to the new settlers and obtaining for itself their abundant raw materials; it did not welcome the establishment in the Colonies of competing industries such as glassmaking."[11]

Under these stifling conditions, glassmaking was unable to make more than cursory inroads in the New World. Eventually rampant dissatisfaction with oppressive Colonial regulations culminated in the American Revolution. The newly-formed United States of America was at last free to profitably venture into the business of competitive manufacturing and national and international commerce. For some it was too late, but for others it was the dawn of glorious new opportunities.

Although there was a core of somewhat complex glassmaking during the years preceding and immediately following the war for independence (including several short-lived ones in upstate New York), only wealthy Europeans and Americans could afford glass products beyond necessities like windowpanes and tableware, as well as inexpensive decanters, flasks, and medicine bottles.

Early American cologne bottle of enameled flint glass in a design that appears to be of Pennsylvania German origin.

Almost 7" tall, a rare medium amethyst Loop Pattern flint glass cologne bottle with original stopper.

Rare ruby flash and clear early American perfume bottle in Hobnail pattern.

In addition to oppressive tariffs, another circumstance contributed to the demise of some of the early American glassmakers. Citizens of the newly-formed United States remained enamored of imported glass, most especially those in the heavily-leaded Anglo-Irish style. By comparison, German-style glass was generally fashioned from what was referred to as "soda glass," and was usually embellished with a light engraving. This consumer preference took its toll on many early glassmakers. The only respite was for a brief nine-year period, beginning in 1809, when an embargo was placed on imports. Unfortunately, the embargo occurred too late for many who had ventured into this volatile industry.

There was an "upside" to this grim picture, however, for others were waiting in the wings. Like their German counterparts of decades before, many Irish and English glassmakers now made their way to the United States, giving the industry another opportunity to participate profitably in the American glass market.

As the eighteenth century progressed into the nineteenth, glassmaking in America was expanded geographically, with artisans moving from one establishment to another, either by proferring their skills in new operations, or by contributing their expertise to established manufacturers. By 1850, there were over 120 glass factories, both large and small, in the United States. All were influenced, either directly or indirectly, by the invaluable background supplied by European guilds and the previous generations of individual artisans. Pioneering this effort, and foremost among his peers, was Henry William Stiegel, an eighteenth century icon.

Four examples of American colored glass cologne bottles (left to right): extremely rare 7.5" Amberina-colored with hexagonal design; rare design in ruby, 8.5"; extremely rare dark red Amber, with some areas resembling Amberina coloring, 7.25"; hexagonal amber design, 6.75".

HENRY WILLIAM STIEGEL — PIONEER IN AMERICAN GLASS

*"Compared with contemporary colonial glass,
Stiegel ware is preeminent for its brilliance,
its resonance, its uniformity, its design
and its purity."*[12]

Although only a few authentic fragrance and perfume bottles by Henry William Stiegel can be viewed today—most in very limited numbers in museum settings—no history of the glass and bottle industry in America can overlook his legacy. Not only was he the first American glassmaker to offer mold-blown bottles, including those for scents and perfumes, but his pioneering spirit stands as a hallmark in any recounting of glassmakers in America.

In 1729, Henry William Stiegel emigrated from Cologne, Germany, a city noted for its expertise in glassmaking. Well-educated, Stiegel began his career as a bookkeeper and clerk at his future father-in-law's ironworks in Brickerville, Pennsylvania. Founded by Jacob Huber, Elizabeth Furnace was named in honor of his daughter, who would later become Stiegel's wife.

Following Elizabeth's death in 1758 (shortly after the birth of their second child), Stiegel became one of three partners in the purchase of Elizabeth Furnace from Huber. Within a year he married another Elizabeth, Elizabeth Holz. Under Stiegel's tutelage, the iron foundry expanded its offerings to include innovative cast-iron stoves, which were noted for their multiple and decorative stove plates.

In 1752, Steigel ventured into the area that now comprises the town of Manheim, Pennsylvania (which he, along with six others, is credited with formally founding ten years later). This land was situated in the heart of Lancaster County's lush countryside, an idyllic place that later earned the well-deserved designation of "The Garden Spot of America." It was in this bountiful area, with its hard-working Swiss and German Mennonite immigrants—whose tradition of agricultural skill had been honed in Europe's lower Rhine Valley—that an American heritage of glassmaking began. And it was there that Stiegel's glass works were built.

With great foresight, Stiegel had purchased thousands of acres, which would later provide timber for the fuel necessary in glass manufacturing. Furthermore, "he also cleared lands for the production of the farm crops needed for his workers and livestock."[13] Stiegel's enterprise grew, and soon what later became Manheim was transformed into a world of its own, with mills, blacksmiths, stores, employee houses, and a mansion for "the lord of the manor."

Stiegel had experimented with glassmaking at Elizabeth Furnace, and armed with experience that he most likely acquired before his emigration from Cologne, he appears to have approached his new venture in Manheim with much confidence. The results attest to his unabashed self-assurance. The first glass in Stiegel's new enterprise was blown about 1765, with an advertisement appearing in Benjamin Franklin's newspaper, the *Pennsylvania Gazette*. It was but one of many such ads distributed over a wide area, thus giving Stiegel the distinction of being one of the first manufacturing facilities in the New World to advertise on a "grand scale."

A Stiegel enameled apothecary bottle.

Although called the "Glass House" by locals, the business was originally named Manheim Glass Works, and was later changed to American Flint-Glass Manufactory. (The term "flint glass" is synonymous with the lead content necessary to give fine glass its resonance and brilliance.)

Stiegel's revolutionary mold-blown bottles included not only those for perfume but also those commonly referred to as "smelling bottles," which apothecaries or buyers would then fill with their choice of fragrance, potently laced with ammonia. This potion was used by females of the day when they felt in imminent danger of suffering a "fainting spell" (commonly referred to as "the vapors"). Most probably an exaggerated feminine wile for the benefit of husbands and suitors, this tiny bottle was not only a necessity in the boudoir, but also to tuck within the confines of her reticule. It served her purposes right through the Victorian period but, as times—and women's striving for independence—progressed, "the vapors" seemed miraculously to vanish, along with street-dusting hemlines, corsets, and high-button shoes.

The scent bottle designation in use during this period generally referred to very small bottles of brilliant coloration. Sold in greater quantities, they were more popular than the standard, larger perfume bottles. Cologne bottles, on the other hand, entered the fragrance field much later than the colonial times of Stiegel and his peers, with records placing the date of their manufacture in the United States sometime around 1830. Early colognes were generally diluted to a lesser concentration with alcohol, so cologne bottles were made to hold more than perfume bottles were.

Stiegel's records indicate that in the 1769-1770 period alone his glassworks listed 584 scent bottles in their inventory, as well as 6,214 regular perfumes. Additionally, he was a pioneer in the art of enameled glassware, being the first in America to offer it. Stiegel's engraved glass pieces were masterpieces of artistry as well, with most of them credited to the expertise of one Lazarus Isaacs.

Very decorative, and often in the popular amethyst color, perfume bottles necessitated a plethora of decorative molds. Many of Stiegel's scent and perfume bottles had the added beauty of a diamond-daisy design. This particular daisy ornamentation is solely Stiegel's and is found only on these specialized bottles. "It is made up of a series of diamonds, each one filled with a daisylike flower whose petals conform exquisitely to the lozenge-shaped enclosures. These bottles, which may have been filled with toilet water or cologne for the use of Colonial ladies, were made from a single gather of glass, which gives them a fragile appearance."[14]

The variety of Stiegel's offerings was impressive beyond the scope of anything heretofore seen in America, equaling the quality of their finest European counterparts. (It is interesting to note that Robert Fulton, Sr., the father of the inventor of the steamboat and a Lancaster native, was one of Stiegel's early customers.) But the vagaries of the times also took their toll, and five years after it began, Stiegel's enterprise collapsed under the British burden. Forced into debtors' prison, he was never able to re-establish himself in American glassmaking. Nonetheless, Stiegel's influence extended far beyond the confines of Manheim, for he contributed, both directly and indirectly, to the expansion of the industry, with many of his finest artisans forced to pursue their craft in areas of expanding opportunity elsewhere.

In the late nineteenth century, an influential Manheim native named George Danner founded a private museum there, which he oversaw until his death in 1917. In 1935 Milton S. Hershey, scion of the Hershey chocolate empire, purchased a large collection of Pennsylvania German material from the trustees of the Danner estate, which included most of the Stiegel glass then available for viewing in Manheim. Attesting to the scarcity of authentic Stiegel glass—and most specifically smelling or scent bottles—approximately thirty examples of Stiegel glass are now on view at the Hershey Museum, and of these, only two fall into the scent bottle category, one clear and one purple.

Unfortunately, today "it is only a very experienced connoisseur who can unerringly identify a piece of glass as true Stiegel."[15] Even then, such determination is often questionable and it becomes an unfortunate case of "let the buyer beware." In fact, collections that have been carefully researched have been known to fall into the "dubious" category. Much of this disparity of opinion is due to the fact that Stiegel glass was so like its finest European counterparts that, in some cases, it is virtually impossible to distinguish one from the other. Understandably, any pieces of Stiegel glass yet to be discovered, or procured from authenticated and long-standing personal collections, would command hefty sums today. As an example, in 1946 one of the largest private collections of Stiegel glass, which was the property

This purple scent bottle is in the "daisy in the square" design for which Stiegel was noted.

Heading home . . . . Baron Stiegel's return to the manor, from a painting by Charles X. Carlson.

of a Lancaster resident, was placed on the auction block. An amethyst bottle was hammered down at $900. Other pieces sold for over $600. These were enormous sums in 1948, being the equivalent of two to six months' wages for an average, middle-class family.

Referred to as "Baron Stiegel," this gentleman was, by all accounts, a colorful personality and certainly one of the premier entrepreneurs of his day. His personality seemed to be strongly influenced by the Old World traditions of pomp and ostentation. Although some anecdotes are probably embellished, they nevertheless offer an amusing insight into this ebullient and eccentric man. "It has been said that on the platform atop his Manheim house, a watchman was stationed . . . and it was his duty to watch the distant road for signs of his appearing. As Stiegel travelled about in a coach drawn by four horses with outriders, his coming could be discerned by the clouds of dust occasioned by his baronial equipage. . . . Then . . . the watchman . . . fired the signal cannon, the musicians were ready with appropriate music, the villagers left their homes to assemble in front of the Stiegel home, and so the great man, baron in his accoutrements if not in fact, came home to music by the band accompanied by the cheers of the villagers."[16] For a gentleman so obviously entranced with the limelight, there is much about Stiegel that remains a mystery. There is no evidence that he ever commissioned a portrait, and no known likeness of him exists. The date of Stiegel's death is questionable, and the site of his grave is unknown.

Stiegel left a heritage that extended beyond his legendary glass: the celebrated Festival of the Red Rose, where to this day one red rose (also historically symbolic of Lancaster County) is presented to the direct descendants of Baron Stiegel. In 1772, Stiegel deeded a parcel of land to the Lutherans of Manheim, on which they built a church. "The deed specified that beside the nominal purchase price of five shillings, there was also to be paid to Henry William Stiegel His Heirs or assigns in the month of June yearly hereafter the rent of One Red Rose."[17] In tandem with what is undisputedly some of the most beautiful glass ever produced, the gift of one red rose is a fitting legacy for one of America's most illustrious, and colorful, manufacturing pioneers.

A depiction of the "One Red Rose" ceremony from the June 1898 issue of *The Ladies Home Journal.* The caption reads, "They form in slow procession and drop their roses, one by one, within the chancel rail."

JOHN FREDERICK AMELUNG, THE GALLATIN COMPANY, & THE EXPANSION WESTWARD

Emigrating from Germany in 1784 and backed by a group of German investors, John Frederick Amelung disembarked, well-prepared and intent on establishing a viable glassworks. Not only did Amelung move his family and all his household possessions, but sixty-eight workers also made the journey with him. Like Stiegel, Amelung's group had the foresight to invest in the timberland so vital for fuel and building materials, and, also like Stiegel, he constructed housing for the employees. Before long, over three hundred workers had settled at the factory, situated in a carefully-chosen site several miles outside of Frederick, Maryland. It was called New Bremen, in honor of Bremen, Germany.

The majority of Amelung's pieces were geared solely for use in the kitchen and at the dining table. However, most were distinctive in many areas of the fine glassmakers' art, including engraving, which was generally deeper and more detailed than the engraving found on pieces attributed to Stiegel. Many of these engraved pieces were exquisite presentation pieces, and included everything from elaborate goblet styles to decanters, and even sugar bowls.

In smaller quantities, the New Bremen factory also offered scent bottles, usually in shades of amethyst or blue. Although they had variations of Stiegel's daisy pattern—one in a rare hexagonal daisy style—the design for which they are most noted featured diamonds, not daisies. This is particularly noteworthy for the play of light on its individual diamond segments, each of which was divided into four small blocks, serving to heighten the refraction even further.

Although Amelung's was one of the finest glass houses then in operation, it was nonetheless overshadowed by the earlier Manheim operation of Baron Stiegel. Still, many of Amelung's offerings are breathtakingly beautiful, with detail (especially in the etched and engraved pieces) that cannot fail to inspire awe and admiration for the talents of the artisans who produced them.

This venture, too, was sadly destined for failure. As it did for many of his peers, the 1809 embargo on imports came too late to help Amelung; his business closed in 1795, just ten years after it had opened. However, again like Stiegel, Amelung's legacy involved more than the pieces produced at the New Bremen factory, for he must also be credited with strongly influencing the future of the American glass industry. The first stage of this influence involved the migration of many of his employees to the Pittsburgh and Ohio River valley areas in order to pursue their trade when New Bremen closed. It was such movement that extended workmen and artisans ever outward, like a spider's web.

Among these determined individuals were "a group of former employees [who] entered into partnership with a wealthy young Swiss-American, Albert Gallatin and his brother-in-law James Nicholson, for the construction of a factory at New Geneva, Pennsylvania."[18] Called the Gallatin Company, it was established in 1797. Albert Gallatin had a prestigious political background, having served both as a Congressman and as Thomas Jefferson's Secretary of the Treasury. With much of Gallatin's workforce coming from defunct glass houses, one of their prized employees was Balthazer Kramer, who had previously been employed by both Wistar and

Stiegel. Again, new inroads were forged, for the Gallatin Company marked the first such west of the Allegheny Mountains, with the product quite naturally bearing a strong resemblance to that for which Amelung was noted.

Although shortages of wood contributed to the failure of many early glass houses, it was just such a shortage of timber that contributed to the growth of the glass industry in Western Pennsylvania and West Virginia, for in these areas coal was readily available to provide the necessary fuel. The modernization of the American glass industry was underway!

CASPAR WISTAR, THE STANGER BROTHERS, THE WHEATON FAMILY, & THE LEGACY OF SOUTH JERSEY GLASS

In 1739, a brass button manufacturer of German descent named Caspar Wistar established a glass works called Wistarberg Glass House in New Jersey. Wistar glass was not produced in large quantities, thus differing from the illustrious Stiegel glass to follow. It was Wistar glass, however, that set the standard for what was referred to as "South Jersey glass." Rebelling against colonial oppression, the maverick Wistar gave vent to his frustrations in the following advertisement:

> As the above-mentioned glass is of American manufacture, it is consequently clear of the duties the Americans so just complain of; and at present it seems peculiarly the interest of America to encourage her own manufactures, more especially those upon which duties have been imposed for the sole purpose of raising a revenue.[19]

Unfortunately, the American Revolution was destined to cost Wistar his business. In addition to the economic hardship of war, Wistar's employees laid down their blow pipes for rifles and marched off to fight for freedom in the Continental Army. Compounding this setback, New Jersey itself became the site of many battles and unheavals. Never recovering from the effects of the war, Wistar's glassworks was forced to close in 1781.

Under the aegis of the Stanger brothers, several of Wistar's employees attempted to continue the tradition of South Jersey glass in nearby Glassboro. In a virtual merry-go-round of glassmakers, the Stangers also attracted other former Wistar Glass workers once their factory was established. One of the Stanger's premier employees was the aforementioned Balthazer Kramer, who had also contributed his skills to Amelung, Stiegel, and Gallatin.

Although the bulk of early South Jersey glass was produced for windowpanes, it was blown in much the same way as hollow ware. However, it was blown so thin that the colors of the coarsely textured, sometimes bubbled glass were barely discernible in the panes.

The Revolution did not entirely overcome the influence of the British, however. Even following this unheaval, American glassmakers had difficulty competing with an influx of British imports—especially at the end of the War of 1812, "when

Early American blown molded cologne bottles. The amethyst example in the center is attributed to New England; the remaining were produced by the Williamstown Glass Works in Williamstown, New Jersey between 1840 and 1854. Photograph courtesy of the Museum of American Glass, Wheaton Village, Millville, New Jersey.

British factories lost no time in dumping accumulated stocks of unsold glass on the American market."[20]

There was a basic difference between early South Jersey glass and that produced by Stiegel: "Where South Jersey-type glass was made in an atmosphere where every man was his own designer, Stiegel-type pieces were made in distinctive kinds, in a definite selection of colors and in a specific range of ornamental techniques.... Baron Stiegel ... was determined to provide the American colonies with glass which could rival or replace European imports."[21] In that respect, he was eminently successful.

One of the major New Jersey glass manufacturers during the early and mid-ninenteenth-century period was the Williamstown Glass Works, which produced all manner of bottles for the druggist trade, including patent medicine vials, syrup bottles, packing bottles, and those referred to as "colognes" and "fancy pungents," as well as made-to-order designs. Between 1840 and 1854, advertisements for the "Colognes" (most at $.50 to $1.25 per dozen) offered a plethora of designs with names like Barrel, Cathedral, Dragon, Flower Basket, Harp, Urn, Panelled, and Square Flower. The "Fancy Pungents," all at $.50 per dozen, were in designs with descriptive names like American Eagle, Dolphin, Grapes, Magnolia, and Strawberries.

The Stanger name seems embedded in the history of South Jersey glass, for another gentleman, named Solomon Stanger, was also a South Jersey glassmaker.

He worked out of a modest shop between 1848 and 1852, and was noted for his figurals and (most especially) for bottles in the popular grape design.

Millville, New Jersey is a site to be reckoned with in any recounting of the influence of South Jersey glass. One of the best known factories was founded in 1806 by James Lee, and with several changes of ownership over the ensuing years, the business successfully continues today. Another important site was Harmony Glass Works, founded in 1813. However, both of these operations established their reputations by making items other than fragrance bottles and related accoutrements.

Not to be overlooked—and also located in Millville, New Jersey—is the T.C. Wheaton Glass Company. Founded in 1888, by 1890 it was under the sole ownership of Dr. Theodore Wheaton, a gentleman who was not only a physician but also operated several pharmacies. Joined in 1899 by his son Frank Hayes Wheaton, Dr. Wheaton concentrated mainly on pharmaceutical bottles. In 1935, Frank Wheaton began a modernization and expansion project, which led to the manufacture of fragrance and cosmetics containers for many illustrious parfumers like Matchabelli, Coty, Bourjois and Guerlain, and the factory became the largest supplier of decorative stoppers in the United States. Expanding into two companies shortly after the end of World War II, the newly-formed Wheaton Glass Company carried on this specialization, and is now in its third generation as a family-operated enterprise. Frank Wheaton remained an icon in the business, working until his death in 1983 at the age of 102!

THE NEW ENGLAND INFLUENCE, FROM PITKIN TO THE NEW ENGLAND GLASS COMPANY & THE BOSTON & SANDWICH WORKS

One of the earliest and most renowned glass houses in New England was that of Pitkin in East Hartford, Connecticut, which dates to the 1780s. It was from this name that the term "Pitkin glass" derived. As stark testimony to the pivotal role of timber in early glassmaking, which was so important to pioneers like Stiegel and Amelung, the Pitkin plant was forced to close in 1830 because of a shortage of wood.

Another New England operation was The Coventry Glass Factory Company, located in Coventry, Connecticut. Founded in 1813, it was a relatively long-lived firm, lasting until 1850. One year after its closing, another glass factory opened in West Willington, to remain in business until 1872. (It is interesting to note that the same group that invested in the West Willington operation was responsible for the founding of New York's Ellenville Glass Works in 1836.) There were also small glass operations at Salem and Braintree, Massachusetts, during these early years, as well as a short-lived venture in 1780 by Robert Hewes of Temple, New Hampshire.

The New England Glass Company, founded in 1818 in Massachusetts, was one of the largest and best known. Because it held the patents for an exclusive pressing machine, this company was at the forefront of the pressed glass industry, an application that became the mainstay of New England glass. Many beautiful perfume and cologne bottles were fashioned of pressed glass, as well as numerous other items to beautify the home, such as vases and lamp bases. In contrast to the needs of most of their predecessors and contemporaries, the company wasn't dependent on lumber; like many of their western counterparts, they too found coal to be a viable alternative. Leased to William and Edward Libbey in 1878, the New England Glass Company prospered until a costly strike in 1888 forced them out of business.

The Massachusetts-based Boston and Sandwich Works, founded in 1825 by a former employee of The New England Glass Company, overshadowed the others because of one major, and stunning, application. They became known for their lacy-patterned pressed glass, and the term "sandwich glass" eventually becoming a generic one.

Expertise in pressed glass was not the only "claim to fame" of New England glassmakers. They were also hailed for their decorative bottles. Figurals were particularly popular during this period in all three types of fragrance bottle—perfume, scent, and cologne. These included unusual subjects like fashionably clad ladies, shoes, animals, fish, and faces. One such figural had particularly macabre overtones, featuring, "the embossed face and name of a child, Charlie Ross . . . produced around 1880 [it] commemorates the most famous kidnapping of the nineteenth century. The Ross child was abducted on July 1, 1874 and was never seen again, though his father, a wealthy merchant, spent substantial sums on advertising and rewards. The bottle appears to have been a last, hopeless effort."[22]

Overall, 1888 was a sad year for the glass industry, for it was then that both the New England Glass Company and the Boston and Sandwich Works closed their doors, joining the ranks of many others. Despite the strivings of all these companies, both large and small—and the individuals who founded and nurtured them, like Baron Stiegel, Joseph Amelung, and the Stanger Brothers—by the close of the nineteenth century independent glassmaking in America had essentially come to an end.

From the Victorian period, an apothecary "smelling" bottle fashioned in the New England tradition. Filled with smelling salts, it has a faceted stopper and measures 6.5" x 3". The shield-centered label reads "the Browne Pharmacy, New Bedford, Mass."

Four rare canary yellow cologne bottles (left to right): a hexagonal design by the New England Glass Co.; by the Boston and Sandwich Works; the cane pattern of the New England Glass Co.; a period design by Sandwich. Heights range from 6" to 7.5".

Four cologne bottles (left to right): canary yellow Sandwich "Star and Punty" design; canary yellow decanter or cologne from New England Glass Co.; rare opalescent blue cologne bottle, also of New England origin; Early American cologne of opaque white with white overlay. Heights range from 6.75" to 8".

An example of New England pressed glass. The intricate design on the flat-topped stopper is also reflected on the bottom of the hefty 5.5" bottle.

Of twentieth-century vintage and most likely New England origin, this stylized 7.5" pressed glass perfume is particularly charming for its unusual shape.

Historical Perfumeries & Enchanted Perfumery Replications

What is referred to as pure perfume, or extrait, is generally comprised of twelve to twenty percent of the essence, with the remainder consisting of alcohol and a small amount of distilled water. When the level drops to eight to ten percent, the product becomes eau de parfum. Eau de toilette, commonly referred to as toilet water, is most apt to have just one scent, such as lavender, violet, or rose water, with essential oils then dropping to five to eight percent.

Plants are crucial to perfume, as they "supply aromatic resins, balsams and essential oils. Out of a quarter of a million flowering plants, less than two thousand possess these readily evaporable ingredients and out of this second figure only relatively few are suitable for perfumery."[1]

Synthetic ingredients often play a prominent role in a perfume's complexity as well. Some merely imitate natural scents, while others offer entirely new olfactory pleasures. The latter cannot, as a whole, be dismissed or denigrated, for often they tend to be more expensive and complex than natural ingredients, thereby adding an exciting new spectrum to the art of perfumery.

When that bottle of precious substance is opened, a full spectrum of olfactory sensations comes into play. The first whiff supplies the *note de tête* or "top note." The "middle note," or *note de coeur*, which gives the liquid its character, cannot be discerned until the fragrance has come into initial contact with the skin, and the *note de fond*, or "end note," is the element that lasts after the scent has remained in contact with the skin's warmth. This is the aura that clings, supplying that personal ambiance so variable from one individual to another. To achieve the ultimate melding of three into one is the parfumer's genius, for, carefully integrated, these notes combine to create one harmonious—and heady—whole.

Innumerable perfumeries throughout the world have left a legacy of individualized and ground-breaking contributions. Some are still titillating the public with exciting new scents, others have long since closed their doors. All of these enterprises cannot, of course, be adequately represented in a single book, but a look at the heritage of several will convey the atmosphere that existed during the various time periods of each perfumery's history.

Chosen to be profiled here are single representatives from three major countries. Along with their brethren, each influenced not only the lives of its clientele but the social climate as well. Just as fashion mirrors the times, so too does fragrance. Although in many instances we can no longer revel in the scents, the bottles that housed them continue to forge a valuable link between the past and the present. That link is also strengthened by the French replication, Chamerolles.

CHAMEROLLES~ FROM MEDIEVAL FRANCE, A MODERN~DAY REPLICATION

Now also known as the Château of Perfumes, Chamerolles has a long and impressive history. Originally constructed as a French fortress in the twelfth century and later converted to a chateau, this massive structure was meticulously restored in 1987 by the Loiret Department Conseil Général to serve a dual purpose—it presents in minute detail the Château's Renaissance splendor, while at the same time it incorporates authentic tableaus of the art of perfumery's beginnings, a heritage of which France is justifiably proud.

Surrounded by living quarters and gardens that historically reflect the ambiance of centuries past, visitors to Chamerolles are able to view replications of early advancements in the development of perfume, along with glimpses of the personal use of scent by the Château's early occupants. From room to room and along the garden paths, this journey through a long-ago time and place is aptly called the "perfumed walk."

The romance and intrigue of knighthood permeates Chamerolles, for Lancelot the First (who later changed his surname to Du Lac) was named after one of the most famous Knights of the Round Table. Lancelot the First was "governor of Orleans and familiar with Kings Louis XII and Francois I, with whom he fought in the Wars of Italy," and "had the present chateau rebuilt from 1500 to 1530."[2] The Du Lacs were succeeded by the Saumery, Coetlogon, Lambert, and Brossard families between 1672 and the end of the nineteenth century. It is to the credit of all that the orginal architectural concept of the chateau was never altered. Its appearance remains as it was intended . . . a medieval fortress replete with moat, round towers and few external window openings. The buildings that face the internal courtyard had little to suggest the military facade that surrounded them, serving as pleasant living quarters for the nobles. As one writer remarked, "the effect of the facades with their black and red bricks, the lead ornaments on the crest of the roof, and the sculptures on the window gables, enhances an architectural form which reflected a new style of living."[3]

Each wing maintains its own individual charm. To the north are the pigeon loft, stables, and saddlery, which sharply contrast against the elaborate vestibule and dining room, both in the style of Charles X. On the clay paving stones stand six busts from the collections of Cardinal de Richelieu. The windows of the west wing provide light to the Renaissance-style living quarters, with salons that retain their original sixteenth- and seventeenth-century decor. The northwest tower at one time served as the quarters of Guillaume Lambert, Louis XVI's Financial Controller. The south wing has galleries and a staircase tower containing the coats of arms of King Louis XII. Less heraldic, but nonetheless impressive for its adherence to historical detail, the kitchen has a Renaissance fireplace and double hearth. The chapel is situated in the southwest tower, its imposing throne inscribed with the oldest example of Huguenot inscriptions to be found in France. With its sculptured frame, the chapel door remains in near-perfect original condition and is an outstanding example of early sixteenth-century architectural embellishments.

It is amid these imposing surroundings that we find the "perfumed walk." Here one can journey through the original settings and observe the developments that had such enormous impact on the art of perfumerie. Ushered in during the Renaissance, these advancements involved distillation, large-scale alcohol production, and the printing of the first perfume recipe books. Each was destined to have a major, long-term effect on the creation of scents— for example, "distillation made it possible to produce perfumes which were no longer oil- or water-based but alcohol-based, and to extract the perfumed essences of the plants using relatively simple procedures. The printing of the first recipe books in Venice made it possible to distribute techniques and products throughout Europe."[4] A scholar's workroom contains the documents, products, and equipment—including mortars, plant presses, and raw materials—necessary to the work of a sixteenth-century perfume maker. Adjacent to it is a laboratory, outfitted with the requisite furnace and glass equipment to complete the distillation process. Progressing from formulas to production to actual application, the bedchamber offers an opportunity to glimpse the many ways in which scents were utilized throughout the chateau, including such innovative accents as attaching aromatic plants to the beams.

Interest in flowers and fragrances became even keener in the seventeenth century. So fierce was the competition to possess the rarest and most sought-after flowers that this century produced a "war" that involved petals, not weapons! It was called the "War of the Tulips," and any means (be they fair or foul!) were used to gain possession of the most desirable tulip bulbs before being outmaneuvered by one's horticultural competitor. A stroll through Chamerolle's lush gardens is colorful testimony to the continuing influence of flowers and fragrances.

Hygiene and seventeenth-century medicinal beliefs played a somewhat dubious role in the history of perfume. One of Chamerolle's rooms is devoted to a strange abberation. Because water was thought to be detrimental to one's health, "dry washing" was undertaken in chambers especially designed for that purpose, with perfume-soaked linens substituting for the proverbial "Saturday night bath." The eighteenth century ushered in a more enlightened view of hygiene; the joys of bathing again came into favor, with scent considered as complementary to the bath rather than as a substitute for it!

The Enlightenment saw expansion in the discovery of new European scents. It wasn't until the nineteenth century, however, that the perfume industry had its formal beginnings. Chamerolle's historical panorama progresses to a reconstructed perfume "shoppe" of that era, replete with collections ranging from simple flasks to hollow walking sticks.

As the Chamerolles guidebook explains, "the 20th century was when the perfume bottle came to be very closely associated with the perfume itself. The Chamerolle collection combines prestigious bottles with those which Daum, Lalique, Murano, Saint-Louis, Baccarat, etc. manufactured for perfume or perfume clothes designers, such as Coty, Guerlain, Lancome, Roger et Gallet, Poiret, Chanel, Lanvin and Dior."[5]

Although Chamerolle was constructed "to fortify and not glorify," it seems an apt environment in which to re-create the ambiance of earlier times in the evolution of perfume . . . one that can rarely be viewed in such historically authentic and impressive surroundings.

CROWN PERFUMERY

Founded in 1872, London's Crown Perfumery Company was on the "cutting edge" of the Victorian era, as evidenced by their flagship product *Crown Lavender Smelling Salts*. Ironically, *Lavender Smelling Salts* was formulated by William Sparks Thomson, whose father manufactured Royal crinolines and corsets. Thus, when ladies of the day fainted because of the breathtakingly tight garments provided by the elder Thomson, they were revived by *Lavender Smelling Salts* formulated by his son!

Following in the wake of its ever-popular smelling salts, Crown Perfumery's first actual scent was *Crab Apple Blossom*, a refreshing and welcome alternative to many of the headier scents then in vogue. The introduction of *Crab Apple Blossom* marked the beginning of an enormous rate of growth. By 1879, Crown was at the forefront of the Victorian socio-industrial movement, selling a staggering half a million bottles of *each* of their forty-nine scents, which were marketed in forty-seven countries around the world. Standing as tribute to their dominant position in the field are more than twenty gold medals that Crown was awarded over the years in honor of the quality and presentation of their fragrances.

By the early 1920s, Crown's clientele included such prestigious personages as Queen Victoria and the future Edward VII. Indeed, "from 1872 to the mid-1930s, most of Mayfair wore Crown fragrances (and Edward VIII plied Wallis Simpson with its perfumes)."[6]

Crown *Lavender Room Freshener* in sterling silver basket, circa 1890. Courtesy Crown Perfumery

Advertisement for Crown fragrances, from the May 31, 1912 issue of London's *Daily Mail*. Courtesy Crown Perfumery

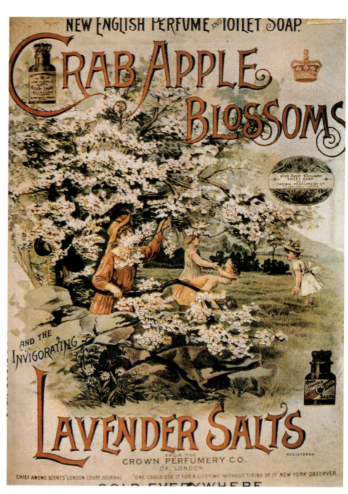

Vintage Crown advertisements. Courtesy Crown Perfumery

The magnificent Crown Baccarat Crystal Flacon, currently produced from the original mold in a limited edition. Photograph courtesy Crown Perfumery.

The death of its founder and interruption of trade due to the First World War caused a marked decline in Crown's operations, leading to a temporary, albeit six decades, hiatus from British soil. During the period between World Wars I and II, the operation of the Company was in the hands of the Thompson family of New Haven, Connecticut, but later deacquisitioned by one of the Thompson daughters. The Company remained in limbo until 1983, when historical acquisitions—including the original Crown fragrance formulation books—inspired Barry Gibson, a chemist, to begin his ten-year quest to restore the Crown Perfumery to its rightful place in the annals of perfumeries, both past and present. Nearly a decade later—in May of 1994—this enormous effort resulted in the relaunch of The Crown Perfumery.

The rare perfume manuscripts, some dating as far back as the seventeenth century, are the basis of the twenty-six fragrances currently offered by Crown. The bottles are modeled after the original crown-topped one first seen in *Crown Lavender Smelling Salts*, a design that has served as the company's trademark since the beginning. The Crown Baccarat Crystal Flacon (from the original mould) has currently been produced for purchase in a limited collector's edition.

Housed in an elegant London showroom, floral scents with appealing names like *Sarcanthus, Crown Ess,* (purported to be Queen Victoria's favorite), *Crown Bouquet, Matsukita, Crown Heliotrope, Marechale* (created in 1669 for Madame La Marechale D'aumont, and recreated from the original formula book), and its lighter counterpart *Marechele 90,* have successfully restored The Crown Perfumery legend. The results ably reflect the exclusive art of true British perfumery—unique scents hand-blended from the finest natural ingredients and housed in an elegant environment, where clients, while they sip tea or champagne, can sample all twenty-six fragrances.

CARON PARFUMEUR

*"From its founding in 1904,
the house of Caron has always followed
three golden rules from Classic perfumery:
the Head Note represents Tradition,
the Heart note, Innovation
and the Base note, Provocation."*

At the turn of the century, a French gentleman named Monsieur Ernest Daltroff and his friend, Monsieur Kahann, acquired The Parfumerie Emilia. With only two years in which to repay the loan, it soon became apparent that Parfumerie Emilia had little to recommend it . . . tiny premises, only two workers, and few fragrances. In short, this relatively unknown quantity could hardly be expected to singlehandedly attract new customers—a difficult task at best, since scents were difficult to sell at that time and used sparingly or not at all.

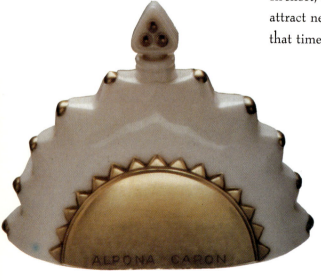

This magnificent bottle held Caron's *Alpona*, launched in 1939. Photograph courtesy Parfums Caron.

The forward-thinking Daltroff began his search for a new name posthaste, and was immediately and—as it would later turn out—propitiously attracted to the name "Magasin Caron," from a perfumery that he spotted on a walk down the Rue Rossini. With the Caron name already spoken for, however, his hopes were dashed. But Fate took over! Returning home that very same day, Daltroff struck up a conversation with a railwayman who boasted of a photograph he had just had taken with his brother, the famous French acrobat, Caron. It was, for Daltroff, synchronicity—and he made up his mind that the old Emilia would become Parfums Caron. This, of course, necessitated a visit to "Magasin Caron," which proved primarily to be a simple haberdashery that concocted individualized perfumes as a sideline. An idea that was once all the rage, scent personalization was now falling from favor. Conditions were ripe for "striking a deal," and Daltroff had little difficulty convincing the owner, Anna-Marie Caron, to join with him and Kahann in a new venture. On August 1, 1903, Parfumerie Caron became a reality. Planning to actively participate in the business for only another year, Anna-Marie Caron's single request was for one percent of the firm's sales for the next five years.

Daltroff's research into the perfume business began in earnest. His venture, however, was blessed with an enormous advantage: "The 'nose,' the name given to someone with a gift of distinguishing different aromas, became a profession . . . Daltroff possessed such a 'nose.' . . . If all the 'noses' were counted throughout the history of perfumery, since the beginning of this century until the present day, we would be astonished to find how few there have been."[7] In Caron's history, there have been only three such "noses" in nearly a century. Thus, Caron perfumes have been overseen by a harmonic synchronicity, much like that which magnetically attracted Daltroff to the Caron name in the first place! It is understandable then that the company's modern-day "nose," Monsieur Lefort, "in his search for a new scent, always asks himself whether it will be faithful to the 'legend.' Will it be a true descendant bearing a family likeness?"[8]

A flapper's dream . . . Caron's inimitable *Bellodgia*. The classic bottle was designed by Félicie Vanpouille. Introduced in 1927, it measures 3" x 2.25".

Caron's *Fleurs De Rocaille*. A lacy "ruff" surrounds the floral stopper, which echoes the box design. Introduced in 1933. 2-5/8" x 2.5"

Photograph courtesy Parfums Caron.

Presented in a black velvet case, the crystal bottle for Caron's *Or et Noir* is lined with 24K gold. The stopper is shown in close-up detail. Circa 1949. Courtesy Dennis Caron

In a delicate blend of orange-blossom, jasmine, and amber, Caron's *Acasciosa*, introduced in 1924. 7.25"

Daltroff was the founding father of this familial line of Caron fragrances. An area that he visited often was Grasse, in southern France—a perfect spot for the cultivation of all manner of flowers and herbs. Foremost, Daltroff needed a "note" upon which to base his first, and future, perfumes, and in 1904 launched two trademarked scents, *Royal Caron* and *Radiant*. Other early scents included *Modernis*, *Ravissement*, and *Chantecler*.

Daltroff's good fortune in "making the right choices at the right times" continued, for he was destined to cross paths with Félicie Vanpouille. She would play a major role both in the future of Caron and in Daltroff's personal life. Circumstances—and undoubtedly fate—had led her to Paris, and also to the establishment of her own dressmaking business on the fifth floor of the building that also housed Parfum Caron . . . 10 rue de la Paix. "On the staircase, he had often passed this proud, beautiful young woman. He would raise his hat, but with never so much as a glance from her in exchange . . . Daltroff was smitten and resolved to conquer the young modiste."[9] With such good luck, who could doubt his success?

Their courtship began soon after, and Vanpouille's artistic abilities and strong business sense became immediately apparent. Indeed, it was Vanpouille who designed the packaging for *Chantecler*. Her influence grew, as Daltroff relied first on her opinions and then on her artistic expertise. Vanpouille also possessed an inherent knowledge of the power of words, which, combined with a flair for public relations, made her services even more invaluable. Although they never married, Daltroff introduced Félicie to his staff as Madame Daltroff, and she used the name from that time forward.

By 1909, Daltroff had purchased the remaining share of Caron from Kahann, and the five year agreement with Anna-Marie Caron had expired. With considerable influence from Vanpouille and a factory at Asnières, the business flourished, offering scents like *Narcisse Noir*, created in 1911, *Rose Précieuse* and *Jacinthe Précieuse* introduced in 1910 and 1911, and the spicy *L'Infini,* trademarked in 1912.

Powders also became part of the Caron repertoire, the first being *N'aimez que moi,* which was available in a choice of three scents—rose, iris, or violet. Later, during the feminine yet freedom-loving era of the 1920s, 1930s, and 1940s—when powdering the nose became almost synonymous with femininity—Caron's *Peau Fine* powder line was hugely successful.

Marking the end of World War I, two French perfumers, Coty and Caron, were invited to participate in a special competition in the United States, which was offering "a reward for the most go-ahead, original and up-to-date firm." Félicie accompanied Daltroff, and her flash of inspiration for decorating the banquet hall once again proved her genius. "Crystal bowls were placed on the dining tables, full of sweet peas, and she arranged for rose petals to be showered over the amazed

Introduced in 1993, *Fleur de Rocaille* by Caron follows in the footsteps of its illustrious predecessor, *Fleurs de Rocaille,* which was introduced in 1933, exactly fifty years earlier. Photograph courtesy Parfums Caron; photographer, Patrick Chaudanson.

Inspired by the request of a Hollywood movie mogul, Caron's *Bain De Champagne*, a current bottle based on the 1941 design. Photograph courtesy Parfums Caron.

Although first introduced in 1949, *With Pleasure* was re-launched in the U.S. in 1984. Photograph courtesy Parfums Caron.

guests, while the whole room was sprayed with the scent of *Narcisse Noir*."[10] With such an act of showmanship, it's not surprising that Caron emerged victorious. The evening's success extended far beyond the banquet hall, for it resulted in a deluge of orders so great that the staff had to be enlarged to accommodate them. Triumphs like these make it clear why Félicie was welcomed as an equal partner in the Caron business.

Foreign sales to North and South America, Eastern countries, and Russia resulted in Caron's surprising lack of concern for the French market. In fact, until 1930, Caron had no French salesmen. Maintaining personal contact with the large emporiums remained Daltroff's responsibility, and even French advertising was considered basically unnecessary. It was even thought that this inaccessibility was *good* for business; "Félicie was convinced that the fact that the products were shrouded in a certain mystery, and that they were not easy to find, gave them a particularly distinguished style."[11] She took this concept to eccentric heights when she offered a discount to any retailer who refrained from displaying Caron products in their windows!

Introduced in 1922, *Nuit de Noel* marked the first Caron scent to achieve a "breakthrough" in the United States. Its notes were of jasmine, ylang-ylang, rose, iris, tuberose, sandalwood, vetiver, and Saxony moss. Its black, cut glass bottle was encircled with a narrow gold band reminiscent of the headdresses so popular with flappers of the era.

Although Félicie separated from Daltroff during this period, later marrying a gentleman named Jean Bergaud, their business partnership remained intact. The split was an emotional blow for Daltroff but had the "upside" of creating a more harmonious atmosphere in the day-to-day workings of the business.

With the "Roaring Twenties" heralding increased freedom for women, change and novelty were inevitable. The volatility of the perfume industry was reflected in the fact that over one thousand perfume names were offered to the public between 1920 and 1935. Nonetheless, these figures did not sway Caron from its intended niche in the industry. Félicie remained convinced that the Caron name should settle for nothing less than "classic" status, as a means of carrying them from one decade to the next. Her instincts were correct. The floral scents, so important a part of Caron's repertoire, were indeed more popular with the busy modern woman than many of the "heavier" fragrances of the past. Madame Bergaud would be pleased to know that her firm conviction would resurface in the 1990s, for the 1980s' trend toward stronger scents is once again being overshadowed by lighter florals.

By 1930, sales in France represented thirty percent of Caron's sales worldwide, forcing Daltroff to finally employ salesmen for the Parisian market. Later, "Only those retailers who came in person to Paris or ordered by post were authorized to sell the Parfums Caron, which were then delivered to them by train."[12]

In the wake of expanding Naziism during the 1930s, Daltroff's Jewish name compelled him to flee the country. He sought haven in the United States, and settled in New York City. The exigencies of war made outside assistance imperative in order that the company be considered truly "French" and not subject to Nazi retaliation, even after Daltroff died of cancer in 1941. By terms of the tontine-like arrangement made years before, the business then passed solely into Félicie's hands.

To protect the company from the Nazis, Daltroff and Félicie had found a new owner, Maurice Bataille. Simply a figurehead, he attended few board meetings and left all decisions for Caron's future with Madame Bergaud. Nonetheless, his pres-

CARON

perfumes of quality and distinction

BELLODGIA
FRENCH CANCAN
FLEURS DE ROCAILLE
NUIT DE NOËL
TABAC BLOND
EN AVION

A limited supply imported prior to the severance of communications with France is available through the better stores without increase in price.

A chilling announcement ends this somber, full-page Caron advertisement from *Stage* magazine, December 1940.

A masterpiece, the packaging for Caron's *Parfum Sacre* is indeed a thing of beauty, with the golden bottle set on a pedestal placed ceremoniously at the heart of its creation. Enclosed by a leaf of cellophone, the extract's case spreads open like a fan to reveal the black inner case embossed in gold. The bottle is visible from the outside, its beauty reproduced in heated gold embossing on the packaging. Even the two bees crowning the stopper are sheathed in gold. The Eau de Parfum is in a purified glass flask with crystal stopper, also topped with two bees. With an aura of poetic myth, the back of each box reads: "The very quintessence of rose revealed by musk and myrrh; A suave and mythical spirit contained in a flask gilded in 24 carat gold." Courtesy Parfums Caron

In appealing designs certain to capture the attention, *Bain Sacre* luxury body care products to complement the *Sacre* fragrance line, launched by Caron in 1994. Courtesy Parfums Caron.

Photograph courtesy Parfums Caron.

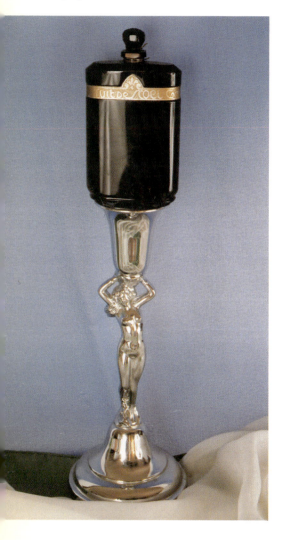

In keeping with its Art Deco origins, the darkly mysterious *Nuit De Noel* by Caron. Introduced in 1922, the gold band adds a "flapper" touch. 4.25"

A stunning bottle for Caron's *Muguet De Bonheur,* based on its 1952 design. Photograph courtesy Parfums Caron.

ence provided Caron with the security it needed and kept the ethnic credentials of the business free from questioning. Bataille had been secured as their "white knight" by German-born Walter Hummelshein, a gentleman who had vast knowledge of perfumery through his association with an American pharmaceutical company. History notes that "Walter Hummelshein was later arrested by the Gestapo for intelligence with the enemy. He was interned at Buchenwald and even there managed to help save many Frenchmen from torture and death! Once liberated at the end of the war, he returned with them to France, a hero."[13]

During the late 1930s and '40s, new scents were created for Caron. Undoubtedly the most unusual in origin, *Royal Bain de Champagne,* introduced in 1941, was the result of a Hollywood tycoon's somewhat ostentatious request. Taken aback by the expense of the champagne baths in which he regularly indulged, he asked Caron to create a scent that could be added to his bath as a suitable replacement!

In a more serious vein, Caron fragrances were responsible—in a most unusual way—for preventing eight Caron workers at the Asnières factory from being forced into *Service du Travail Obligatore* in Germany, a "Compulsory Work Service, imposed during the Occupation on certain categories of the French population." Morsetti, Caron's "nose" at the time, took matters into his own hands. "He had contacted a German commanding officer he had noticed in his usual restaurant. It was not difficult to find which bribe would suit him. After he had been offered the most expensive Caron perfumes, no more was heard of the order to proceed abroad."[14] That ended the work service threat and saved eight employees from foreign servitude . . . and possible death.

With business expanding after the liberation of France, Madame Bergaud realized that attracting foreign buyers to Paris could only be accomplished by larger quarters. Her choice, No. 10 Place Vendôme, fulfilled not only that need, but was also personally prophetic, since she considered ten to be her lucky number!

The new quarters were sumptious indeed. The main reception area featured a staircase leading to the main floor. Beauty salons, replete with dressing tables laden with Caron beauty products, covered over five thousand square feet alone. Cozy yet opulent, the salons provided a peaceful sanctuary where women could meet and socialize while they sampled old favorites and new Caron products. One of the rarest of Caron's bottles, with only a few thousand produced, was launched during that heady period. Introduced in 1949, it contained *Or et Noir.*

In certain key areas, Madame Bergaud's determination never wavered. Among these were her unorthodox ideas regarding the role of salesmen, and the illusory image of Caron products that she chose to portray. "One of her six salesmen, Monsieur Nègre, was an ambassador in the true Caron style. He would arrive at the retailers with his white kid gloves and a silver-knobbed cane . . . and he always insisted on a saleswoman opening the door to invite him in, otherwise he would pass by without entering!"[15] The term "order book" was not in this emissary's lexicon, and his mood alone dictated which retailer would be favored and which would not!

Unlike many of her contemporaries during the 1950s, Madame Bergaud refused to offer new fragrances solely for the sake of doing so, preferring to launch scents only intermittently, relying, as in the past, on the strength of Caron's classics. In April 1952, she did request that Morsetti put his hand (and nose) to a new fragrance. The result was *Muguet du Bonheur*, one that Morsetti concocted in less than a month's time. The bottle was by Bacarrat, and Madame Bergaud, with her usual flair, fell upon the charming idea of decorating its neck with a sprig of artificial lily of the valley.

With her husband in failing health, Madame Bergaud chose to devote most of her time to him. Jean Bergaud died in 1962. The business was sold to Jean-Paul Elkann shortly thereafter, and Madame Bergaud retired at age ninety. She died in 1967 at the age of ninety-four.

Grounded in metallurgy, Elkann was a seasoned businessman. Times had changed, and he quickly sensed that Caron also needed refurbishing. Salons were no longer in favor with busy women, and Place Vendôme was sold. Elkann's appraisal also determined that "the only positive element was the management of the Caron Corporation in the United States, which was run independently, manufacturing its products on the spot, after adapting them to suit the American market."[16] The resultant updating of the French operation attracted prospective purchasers for the Caron business. None interested Elkann until he was approached by the Robins family of Richmond, Virginia, and his arrangement with them marked France's first takeover bid, with the deal finalized in 1966. The Robins group, however, had total confidence in Elkann's expertise, and he remained in control as managing director.

New scents became a major priority. Elkann wasted little time in selecting one that was totally different from any that preceded it. *Infini* was a combination of fragrant florals—tuberose, lily of the valley, and hyacinth, which formed the base—combined with undertones of vetiver and sandalwood. Mindful of the increasing importance of packaging amid the escalating competition, Elkann solicited a contemporary "space age" design by Serge Mansau. The result was "a bottle with asymetrical lines whose angles seemed in defiance of classical geometry."[17]

At that time, members of Caron's board of directors included prominent figures like Nadine and Alain de Rothschild. Assisting Elkann at Maison Caron, and a major player in revitalizing the firm, was François Castex, formerly with Guerlain and well-versed in public relations. Castex left the business in 1975, and Jean-Paul Elkann followed four years later.

The new president of Caron was no stranger to the fragrance field. His name was Henry Bertrand. Of French birth, Bertrand's mother was English and he shared in the cultures of both countries. Working initially for *Vogue* magazine as assistant to the chairman, by the age of 29 he had risen to managing director of Conde-Nast in France. In 1969 Bertrand was offered the managing directorship for Elizabeth

Three sizes of Caron's *Nocturnes*. The tallest stands 6.75". Introduced in 1981. Marked "HP 4, Made in France" (Pochet et du Courval).

For men . . . Caron's *Pour Un Homme*. Photograph courtesy Parfums Caron.

Arden, which had been under the aegis of the elderly Vicomtesse de Maublanc until her death a short time before. Bertrand remained with Arden for five years, at which time he accepted the position of managing director of Jean Patou, where he continued until Caron beckoned in 1979.

Recognizing the need for further growth through investment and change, Bertrand "met Lefort, the 'nose' from Asnières, and asked him to compose an eau de toilette, in accordance with a recent vogue. The former bottle used to present *Pois de Senteur* was brought out again."[18] The scent was appropriately named *Eau de Caron* and made its debut in March 1980. The next year another was introduced, this time of a more sophisticated bent. With a base of Malagasy jasmine and a bottle designed by Pierre Dinand, the fragrance was launched in 1981. Its name was *Nocturnes* and it became another resounding success story in the Caron repertoire, for by 1984 this one fragrance alone represented a third of their sales.

Once again, obsolescence reared its head. With the Place Vendôme setting a thing of the past, Caron's image once again needed bolstering. When its doors opened in March 1982, the new Caron shop on the Avenue Montaigne enchanted the populace with its neo-classical columns, Carrare marble, canopies decorated with gold leaf, and crystal urns by Baccarat. The ambiance was so successful, in fact, that shops of similar style followed in major cities in the United States.

In 1993, an updated version of *Fleurs de Rocaille* was introduced. The only name change was in the first word, with *Fleurs de Rocaille* becoming *Fleur de Rocaille*. More than sixty years after the original scent had been introduced, *Fleur de Rocaille* was formulated to meet the needs of the modern woman while remaining mindful of the ever-present link to its 1933 counterparts. With a bottle designed by Joel Desgrippes, the formula retains the original violet, rose, and lilac floral notes updated with an infusion of gardenia and the warmer, intense bottom notes of sandalwood, cedarwood, and amber.

Parfum Sacre is Caron's latest offering, launched exclusively at Harrods in London and from there to leading stores in 1994. Adding another touch of opulence to the Caron heritage, this fragrance is but part of an expanded line that also includes luxury body care products called *Bain Sacre*.

Thus, the legacy of Caron continues in the tradition so carefully prepared by Monsieur Daltroff and Félicie Vanpouille those many years ago. Long may it prosper!

Launched in 1970, Caron's *Infini* in two sizes of a very stylized design. The smaller 3.25" bottle has an open crystal stopper and the illusion of a see-through cut-out in the base. Although solid, it is cleverly fashioned to hold fluid only in the surrounding areas. The large bottle is 5.25" x 4.5" with an Art Deco stopper in an open-cut design and is marked "Caron, Made in France, VB" (Verreries Brosse); the smaller bottle has the HP (Pochet et du Courval) designation.

ELIZABETH ARDEN... AN AMERICAN ICON

Elizabeth Arden, one of America's premier cosmetic entrepreneurs, emigrated in 1908 from Canada to New York City, where she became a bookkeeper for Squibb Pharmaceutical Company. Trained as a nurse, this certainly was not a perfect match of talent and position, but it was in this environment that Miss Arden's interest in the research and product development side of the business was piqued. Combined with her earlier training, it led to her next position, this time in a beauty salon, where her talents at mixing and applying facial treatments came to the fore.

Arden's ensuing success, fueled by her unwavering determination, is amazing in light of the strongly male-oriented business climate of the early twentieth century. Just two years after her arrival in New York (in what was surely a "man's world") she had chosen her niche, and the flagship Elizabeth Arden salon opened its doors on prestigious Fifth Avenue. It marked the first in a string of worldwide Elizabeth Arden salons, eventually providing skin care and cosmetics in both the United States and abroad. Recognizing the burgeoning opportunities to be found not only in satisfying the beauty needs of the modern woman but also her overall well-being, the salon concept led to the opening of a resort spa named "Maine Chance." Located in the state in which Arden had one of her homes, it was followed twelve years later by another in Phoenix. The luxurious spas were but one of Miss Arden's trend-setting ideas, for she continued to remain devoted to developing cosmetic and skin care products and new makeup styles until her death in 1966. During her years in the industry she remained instrumental in product development as well as the increasingly vital areas of sales promotion and packaging.

The Elizabeth Arden Company has remained dedicated to the precepts of its founder. Its 1971 acquisition by Eli Lilly & Co., the pharmaceutical giant, provided ready access to an outstanding scientific research resource. In 1987, Elizabeth Arden was acquired by Faberge, enhancing their reputation for innovation even further. Today, the company is part of the international Unilever Prestige Personal Products.

This delightful figural is for *Mémoire Chérie* ("Cherished Memory") by Elizabeth Arden. Monsen and Baer Perfume Bottle Auction.

By Elizabeth Arden, the enduring *Blue Grass*, here in *Blue Grass Flower Mist*, 5"; *Blue Grass Hand Lotion*, 5"; and a 4.5" box of *Blue Grass Dusting Powder* topped with its specialty soap. Photograph courtesy Sharon and Howard Weatherly.

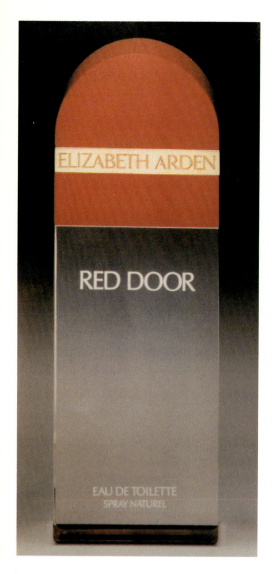

On the red door . . . Elizabeth Arden's *Red Door*, launched in 1989.

Always on the cutting edge, even jet-age technology has been used to develop new Elizabeth Arden products. Indeed, to micropulverize powder, a jet engine at the speed of Mach 2 was set in motion, resulting in a jet-milling process that gave face powder the feel of suede! In a joint program with the Linus Pauling Institute of Science and Medicine, Arden's "Spa Skincare" was launched in 1994. Dedicated to researching the effects of vitamins and minerals, the Institute's study augurs well for future benefits in skin care . . . and future innovative concepts from Elizabeth Arden.

Naturally, this legacy of devotion to the beauty of women wouldn't be complete without fragrances, a fact that was not lost on Elizabeth Arden! In fact, fragrance must have been high on her list of client necessities, for *Velva* was offered shortly after her first salon opened. It was followed by *Cupid's Breath* and *Carnival* in 1916, and *June Geranium* a year later.

The "Roaring Twenties" brought scents like *Arden Jasmin, Arden Rose, Italian Lilac, Brise d'Orient*, and a series with French-inspired names, *La Jardin d'Elizabeth, la joie d'elizabeth, l'amour d'elizabeth, Le Bouquet d'Elizabeth, le êve d'elizabeth, I élan d'elizabeth*, and *L' Etoile d' Elizabeth*.

The 1930s ushered in the timeless scent of *Blue Grass*, an enduring favorite introduced in 1934, along with a host of others sporting intriquing names like *Black Lace, For Her, It's You, Nothing Sacred, Corsage, Ma Rue, Prince's Feather, Tuberose d'Elizabeth, Cyclamen, Box Office*, and the book- and movie-inspired *Gone with the Wind* and *Miss Jezebel*.

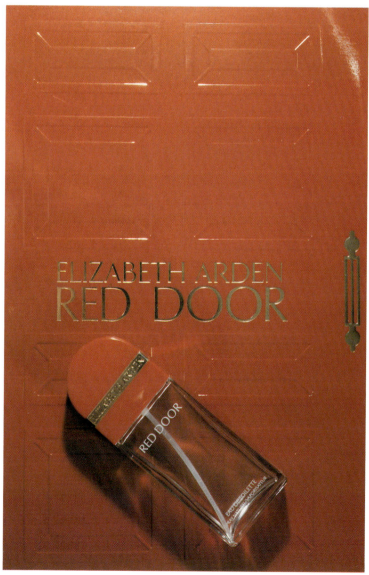

 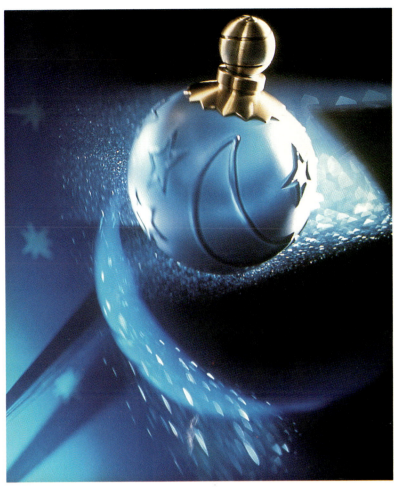

Karl Lagerfeld's design drawing for *Sun Moon Stars* . . . and the glorious bottle that followed. Both courtesy of Elizabeth Arden Company.

Blackout and *Winged Victory* were among the Arden fragrances that reflected the war years of the 1940s. Others introduced in the 1940s included *Eau de France, Lady in Black, Ladies and Gentlemen, Millie Fleurs, Mon Amour, On Dit, My Love, Profile, Surprise, Thousand Flowers,* and *Mountie*. The parade of fragrances continued into the post-war fifties, which saw the launching of *Mémoire Chérie* and *Younger Set*.

In the mid-1970s, Elizabeth Arden extended the perfume line to include what are referred to as "prestige fragrances." Its first such venture occurred in the mid-1970s with the Paris-based House of Chloé and its designer, the renowned couturier Karl Lagerfeld. *Chloé* was the flagship result of this collaboration, and remains an enduring fragrance success. It was followed by *Lagerfeld* and *KL Homme,* both for men, and *KL* for women, as well as *Lagerfeld Photo,* also for men, which was launched in 1990. *Chloé Narcisse*, introduced in 1992, became the second House of Chloé fragrance.

In the 1980s, Arden's joint venture with Italy's Fendi sisters resulted in *Fendi*, and *Fendi Uomo*, along with the Oriental fragrance *Fendi Asja*. In the latter part of the decade, Elizabeth Arden joined forces with another famous Elizabeth . . . Elizabeth Taylor. The result was *Elizabeth Taylor's Passion,* followed in 1991 by the explosive launch of *White Diamonds*. Ranked as the number one fragrance for that year, it continues to maintain its worldwide success. Three additional fragrances were added to the Elizabeth Taylor line in 1993, *Diamonds and Emeralds, Dia-*

monds and Rubies, and *Diamonds and Sapphires.* Another prestige collaboration took place in 1993, this time with the legendary couturier Valentino, resulting in scents for women and men, *Vendetta* and *Vendetta Pour Homme.*

Not inclined to rest on the laurels of past successes and their prestige line, the Elizabeth Arden Company continued to pursue their own new fragrances during this period. *Red Door,* which was a natural outgrowth of the famous "red door" that became the signature entrance to Elizabeth Arden salons, was launched in 1989. *Sunflowers* followed in 1993, a fragrance that readers of *Glamour* magazine ranked among the top ten fragrances a mere month after it reached fragrance counters! In 1995, *Sunflowers* was also named one of the top one hundred U.S. marketing successes by *Advertising Age* magazine. Following closely behind is Arden's latest offering, *True Love,* which promises to garner its own share of accolades.

With such an impressive parade of fragrances and bottle designs spanning decade after decade—for their own as well as the "prestige" lines—its not surprising that numerous "Fifi Awards" (perfumes' equivalent of the Oscars) have been bestowed on Elizabeth Arden by the Fragrance Foundation.

Shakespeare penned the sentiment "O! stay and hear; your true love's coming," and Elizabeth Barrett Browning, "Whoever loves true life, will love true love." Here, Elizabeth Arden's response, *True Love,* introduced in November 1994. Photograph courtesy Elizabeth Arden Company.

Elizabeth Arden's award-winning *Sunflowers,* introduced in May 1993, features crisp, clean graphics in a understated yet romantic design. The bottle has a matte white cap and is decorated with a stylized yellow flower. The sleeves that slide over the carton are printed in two colors, one side yellow, the other white. When lined up together, the front and back merge to create an entire sunflower in two colors. As a final touch, this love note is printed in matte copper ink on the sides of the container: "And the sun was shining when he held me and I felt a deep flowering of pleasure. All at once. Like a sunflower. Opening up." Photograph courtesy Elizabeth Arden Company.

A crowning masterpiece . . . Elizabeth Taylor's *White Diamonds,* an award-winning masterpiece designed and produced by the Elizabeth Arden Co., with the fragrance developed by Clare Cain, Arden's Vice President of Packaging Development. The retail parfum presentation, which mirrors the heavy crystal, pear-shaped bottle designed by Susan Wacker, is crowned with a pavé rhinestone bow containing over three hundred stones. It is presented in a velvety black jewelry pouch inside a matching box. Photograph courtesy Elizabeth Arden Company.

The young woman who came to the United States in 1908 was a pioneer. That Elizabeth Arden's entrepreneurship had profound societal implications, which also had an impact on the enormous growth and change the country experienced after the turn of the century, is attested to by the award posthumously given her in the early 1990s when she was named to *Life* magazine's list of the "Most Important Americans of the 20th Century."

Referred to by today's Elizabeth Arden Company as "Elizabeth Arden, the Woman, the Company, the Legacy," Elizabeth Arden would be proud of their current appraisal of this American success story and the continuation of the legacy she left behind: "Through nearly nine decades, and ahead into the future, the Elizabeth Arden name represents the best of all worlds, combining tradition with technology, elegance and innovation." Today's women, their mothers, grandmothers, and even great-grandmothers would heartily agree!

In its very rare box, Elizabeth Arden's *Cyclamen*, bottle by Bacarrat. Monsen and Baer Perfume Bottle Auction.

Elizabeth Tayor's latest fragrance, *Black Pearls*, introduced in 1996. Photograph courtesy Elizabeth Arden Company

MASTERPIECES IN MODERN GLASS

Garniture DeToilette Aux Liserous en Verre, Double De Gallé, circa 1900. Artist, Ivanhoe Gadpaille

Vaporisateur En Verre É Maillé, De "Daum Nancy," circa 1900. Artist, Ivanhoe Gadpaille

THE GENIUS OF RENÉ LALIQUE

René Lalique was born in France in 1860. His artistic bent became apparent early on, beginning with his fascination with goldsmithing and the knowledge he acquired in this field during his apprenticeship as a youth. His progress was rapid. By the age of eighteen, Lalique had journeyed to London to continue his studies, returning to France at age twenty. Already well versed in goldsmithing, he then decided to try his hand at jewelry design, and over the next five years created designs for many auspicious names, including Cartier. Not content to craft under the aegis of others, Lalique established his own atelier, and in short order his reputation gained him both stature and an enthusiastic clientele.

Rapidly acknowledged as an innovator in the emerging Art Nouveau movement, Lalique produced jewelry that was not only groundbreaking in design and technique but equally impeccable in workmanship. Integrating materials that reached beyond the norm, in a field which heretofore concentrated most prominently on precious gems, his genius was in combining not only the precious but also stones of lesser value in unusual combinations of materials. The lesser stones worked well in the concepts of Lalique's Art Nouveau designs, and in such fanciful settings their beauty often surpassed that of their more staid counterparts. The insects, florals, and figurals of Art Nouveau cried out for materials of diverse textures and appearance, and Lalique's approach carried the art of jewelry design to a new plateau.

Antique perfume bottle created by René Lalique in 1912 for *Fougeres*. Photograph courtesy Lalique Parfums.

This antique perfume bottle was created by René Lalique in 1911 for Roger et Gallet's *Cigalia*. Photograph courtesy Lalique Parfums.

Bouchon Cassis, by Lalique (1920).

René Lalique designed this bottle for Molinard's *Le Baiser du Faune* ("the Kiss of the Faun"). Photograph courtesy Monsen and Baer Perfume Bottle Auction.

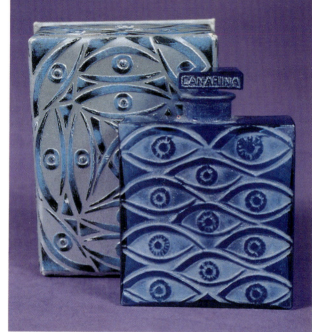

Les Yeux Bleus ("Blue Eyes") by Canarina; produced by René Lalique, it is especially unusual for its intriguing surrealistic design. Photograph courtesy Monsen and Baer Perfume Bottle Auction.

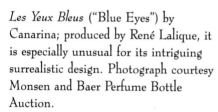

Le Corail Rouge, by Lalique.

In a pleated silk drawstring bag, a frosted miniature marked "Lalique." Courtesy Renee Gold

Significantly, during the 1890s it was this diversification into other materials, and his fascination and experimentation with precious and semi-precious stones, that led Lalique to the equally challenging possibilities to be found in glass. This opened new avenues of artistic applications and subjects. Formerly ordinary objects, like vases, plaques, and figurines, were suddenly being fashioned in most unordinary ways, with experimentation in the design and form of all manner of bottles a natural outgrowth of the trend.

It was then that his association with Francôis Coty, of fragrance fame, began, for fragrance bottles provided a most appropriate subject, wedding the beauty of the bottle to the beauty of its contents. "No overview of the beauty of glass or the mysteries of the scents contained therein would be complete without praise and acknowledgment of the contribution of René Lalique. René Lalique's place in the pantheons of both Art Nouveau and Art Deco design is paramount, but so is his contribution to the modern fragrance industry by way of his handsome glass packaging for scents."[1]

René Lalique and Francôis Coty were pioneers in the early commercial perfume industry — one in glass design, the other in scents — but it was the melding of their talents that brought about a revolution in the perfume industry. Like Lalique's, Coty's influence was far-reaching, even affecting the establishment of other fragrance companies, for the founders of Lancôme, Orlane, and Charles of the Ritz were all his former employees.

By 1909, Lalique's output of perfume bottles warranted the purchase of a glassworks at Combs-la-Ville, near Fontainbleau. The site was well chosen, having long been renowned for the high silica content of the sand. Due to increasing demands, this factory was devoted almost exclusively to the manufacture of commercial perfume bottles. Within the next twenty-plus years, what had started as a one-man operation at Combs-la-Ville had grown to a workforce of over six hundred. During its many years of existence, due to either the stresses of economic conditions or wars, the Combs-la-Ville factory was forced to close on several occasions — once after the start of World War I, again in 1932, and yet again after the outbreak of World War II, which sadly saw the plant occupied by invading German forces.

It was at Combs-la-Ville that precision-cast metal molds, a method devised from the ring mold casting developed by Claude Boucher, were utilized. "Depending on the form of the vessel, the technique employed was either *presse souffle* — where the glass was blown into a hinged double mold . . . or *aspire souffle* — which entailed sucking the 'gather' of glass into a mold automatically by creating a vacuum within it."[2]

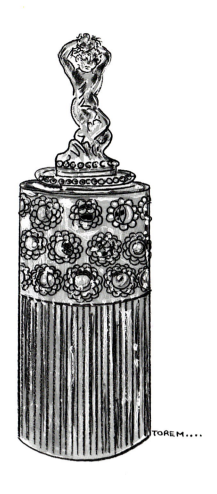

Faune, by Lalique (1930).

Although without identifying label, this spiral topped 2.5" bottle is numbered and marked "R. Lalique," and was designed for Worth's *San Adieu,* circa 1929. Ten years later, Lalique elaborated on this style for Worth's *Imprudence.* 2.5". Courtesy Marilyn Kearney

An etched and painted non-commercial fragrance bottle marked "R. Lalique." 4.5". Courtesy Renee Gold

This set of three dresser bottles in graduated shapes held René Lalique's *Les Perles*. Photograph courtesy Monsen and Baer Perfume Bottle Auction.

This flacon to celebrate the first anniversary of *Le Parfum Lalique* is called "The Four Muses," and was offered in 1994. Photograph courtesy Lalique Parfums.

In 1995, the second anniversary of *Le Parfum Lalique* offered yet another beautiful flacon by Marie-Claude Lalique. On this occasion, it was a floral tribute to its namesake, "Jasmine." Photograph courtesy Lalique Parfums.

During the next year, Lalique began production of decorative bottles into which perfume could be poured by the purchaser, thus offering the owner a permanent dressing table item that could be "recycled" as they depleted the contents of one particular scent and moved on to another. This type of bottle often employed a process called *patine,* a type of enamel used to add color to the recessed areas of the bottle. Carborundum powder was applied to fit the stopper into the bottle. This is a process called *bouchon a l emeri,* "which gives the familiar granular, frosted appearance to neck and stopper and ensures tightness and retrievability. When fitted, stopper and bottle were engraved with corresponding control numbers, which appear on the majority of René Lalique's stoppered vessels, including commercial perfumes, and serve today as useful clues for detecting 'marriages'."[3]

The "tiara" stopper, which is very rare in colored glass, is distinctive to the Lalique-style of design. In some of the more expensive bottles, Lalique favored the very beautiful and appealing black glass. Many of Lalique's toppers were in the form of nymph-like figurals with the look of fine sculpture. These figures were also incorporated into the actual bottle, e.g. his 1914 Sirenes perfume burner with female forms gracefully encircling the bottle. The addition of decorative female figurals added yet another dimension to Art Nouveau's beauty. "Totally lacking in vulgarity, they reflect the spirit of the Belle Epoque and the elegance of the most civilised metropolis of the world."[4]

Lengyel's *Parfum Impérial* in its gold foil box; by René Lalique. Photograph courtesy Monsen and Baer Collection.

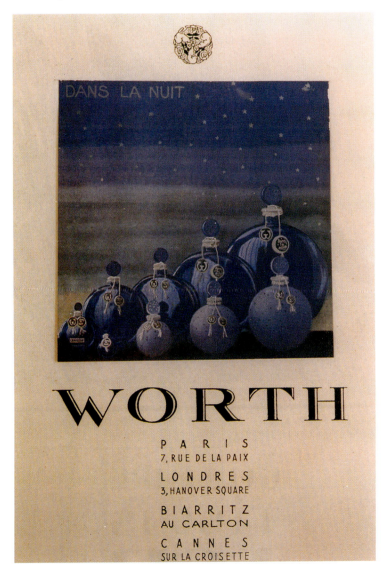

Rare Worth advertisement for *Dans La Nuit,* from *Art, Goût, Beauté,* August 1922. Bottle design by René Lalique.

Vintage atomizer fragrance bottles. The one on right is marked "R. Lalique" in block letters; the bottle at left is unsigned but also in the Lalique style. Both are early twentieth century, and each is marked "BTE SGDG Made in France" on the stopper, "Le Parisien" around the rim, and O.F. indication for "on" and "off." 5.5". Courtesy Renee Gold

Today's masterpiece... For the 1996 Flacon-Collection Edition, Marie-Claude Lalique's "Le Nu," commemorating the third anniversary of the introduction of *Le Parfum Lalique*. Photograph courtesy Lalique Parfums.

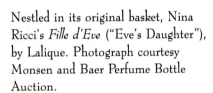

Nestled in its original basket, Nina Ricci's *Fille d'Eve* ("Eve's Daughter"), by Lalique. Photograph courtesy Monsen and Baer Perfume Bottle Auction.

In the Lalique tradition, this magnificent design was created by Marie-Claude Lalique for the 1993 launch of the company's signature perfume. Photograph courtesy Lalique Parfums.

Lalique "produced an uninterrupted stream of flacons during the 1920s, creating 150 designs for at least a dozen parfumers, including Molinard, Houbigant, Coty, D'Orsay, Roger et Gallet, and the House of Worth."[5] In the ensuing years, the list of notables who turned to the Lalique family for many of their bottles grew. Forvil, Lelong, Corday, Lanvin, Fragonard, Arys, Nina Ricci, Isabey, Molyneaux, Caron, Coryse, Veolay, Fioret, deVigny, Jean de Parys, L. T. Piver, the parade of perfume giants goes on and on... just as Lalique perfume flacons go on and on — precious receptacles to be treasured and passed from one generation to another.

One of Lalique's last offerings was for Worth's *Requete* perfume. This design had been undertaken in the late 1930s, but wasn't offered to the public until 1946, probably due to wartime conditions and other extenuating circumstances. The bottle was of full-blown, rounded clear glass with a scallop-style edging highlighted in blue enamel.

As might be expected, the talents of this multi-faceted genius were complex and many-sided. He was the interior designer for Roger et Gallet's perfumerie section, which involved not only the perfume containers but everything from vitrines to furniture. His commercial offerings are an awesome study in contrasts and diversity, covering a vast array of sizes and applications—from tiny scent bottles to entire walls! Indeed, "Lalique was the first glassmaker of the twentieth century to adopt the technique of casting glass blocks for decorative use."[6]

René Lalique died in 1945, and from that time forward the "R" has been eliminated from the identifying signature on Lalique bottles. As Lalique glass during the ensuing years attests, his work proudly continues through the impressive offerings of his son Marc Lalique and granddaughter Marie-Claude Lalique, with over three hundred bottle designs credited to the combined talents of these three generations.

Lalique bottles of the 1990s are a magnificent testament to their founder. In 1993, Lalique's signature fragrance, *Le Parfum Lalique,* was introduced, housed in a beautiful bottle designed by Marie-Claude Lalique. Every year, in celebration of the anniversary of the launch of *Le Parfum Lalique,* Marie-Claude introduces a new, limited-edition flacon. Preceded by the first limited-edition flacon, *Flacon Collection Edition 1994* — "Four Muses," and the second limited-edition flacon, *Flacon Collection Edition 1995* — "Jasmine," the third anniversary bottle, *Flacon Collection Edition 1996* — "Le Nu" will also be available in limited quantities. The elegant 1996 "Le Nu" houses three precious ounces of *Lalique Parfum* in a special limited-edition bottle featuring an exquisite figural stopper inspired by Aphrodite, the legendary Greek goddess of love and beauty. The strength and beauty of each of Madame Lalique's designs are brought to impeccable fruition by the consummate craftsmanship that has been the hallmark of every piece bearing the Lalique signature.

As the beauty of Lalique glass in the years since 1945 attests, the honored name of René Lalique is destined to live on through the magnificent offerings of the present, the as-yet-unseen treasures of the future . . . and always, the glorious bottles of the past!

A 1919 offering, this René Lalique creation was for *Fleurs De Pommier.* Photograph courtesy Lalique Parfums.

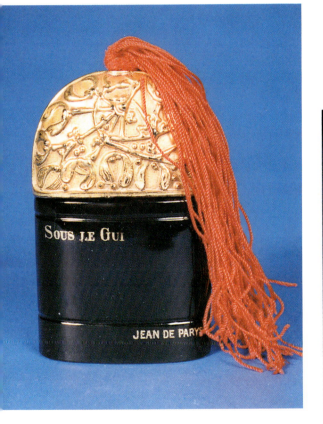

Designed by Lalique, Jean de Parys' *Sous le Gui* ("Under the Mistletoe"). Circa 1924. Photograph courtesy Monsen and Baer Perfume Bottle Auction.

For D'Orsay's *Grace,* designed by René Lalique in 1925. Photograph courtesy Lalique Parfums.

Named after the Greek goddess of the sea and wife of Poseidon, *Amphitrite,* an antique perfume bottle designed by René Lalique, circa 1925. Photograph courtesy Lalique Parfums.

Rigid "side-style" atomizer by DeVilbiss with silvered interior and finely crackled glass. 4.25". Courtesy Renee Gold

DEVILBISS

A blue ribbon for one of the most unusual tales relating to giants in the modern perfume bottle industry must go to DeVilbiss, a company founded in Toledo, Ohio in 1888. Its patriarch was Dr. Alan DeVilbiss. Not a parfumer or chemist but a general practitioner, DeVilbiss invented a bulb atomizer for the purpose of efficiently dispensing his revolutionary nose and throat sprays.

It wasn't until 1907, however, that the elder DeVilbiss permitted his son, Dr. Thomas DeVilbiss, to pursue the idea of utilizing the basic bulb design for perfume flacons, and a patent was obtained in 1910. Innovation at its best, the concept was an enormous success, almost immediately accounting for the bulk of DeVilbiss' business.

For almost fifty years, DeVilbiss perfume atomizers were a treasured accoutrement to boudoirs in both the U.S. and abroad, with the basic bottles and glass supplied by the finest American and European sources. Although still in business today, the company has reverted to the origins of its founder, and now produces only other medical-related and spray-type products.

BACCARAT

A territorial realignment was at least partially responsible for the Baccarat glass so admired today. The tale began around 1800, when the French glass house of Voneche, founded near Givet by M. d'Artigues, found itself no longer in French territory by the terms of the treaty of 1815. M. d'Artigues then "obtained the right of sending his glass duty free for three years into France, on the condition of founding crystal glass works in France during the interval. This he did by buying the glass-house of St. Anne at Baccarat, where up to that time only common glass had been produced, and establishing crystal glass works, which have become the most important of their kind in France."[7]

DeVilbiss Imperial Line atomizer in pink and eggshell blue, decorated with jewels. Photograph courtesy Monsen and Baer Perfume Bottle Auction.

Guerlain's *Coque d'Or* ("Bow of Gold"), blue crystal covered in gold enamel, executed by Baccarat, in its original white box. Photograph courtesy Monsen and Baer Collection.

A bottle measuring 7.75" for Houbigant's *Quelques Fleur*, a fragrance introduced in 1912. A golden center band and stopper and finely executed French court scene encircle the base. The bottle is marked "Baccarat France" and "86."

53

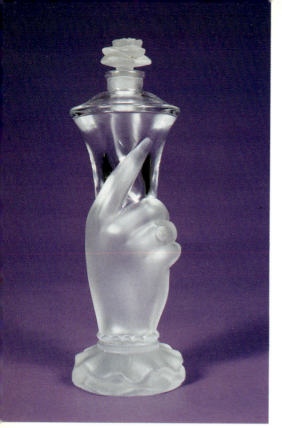

Executed by Baccarat, this frosted hand held Elizabeth Arden's *It's You*. Photograph courtesy Monsen and Baer Perfume Bottle Auction.

With a silvery-gold, deeply etched "sun," this stunningly beautiful bottle was made for L.T. Piver's *Astris*. Although originally launched in 1908, it was again trademarked in the late 1920s. This bottle design, with its double-layered stopper, is a dramatic example of the Art Deco period. Marked "Baccarat, France." 4.5" x 4". Courtesy Marilyn Kearney

Forest, *Ming Toy*, Baccarat (1923).

Thus, although established in 1765, the Baccarat name did not achieve prominence for the exquisite quality of its offerings until d'Artigues' conversion. Early in the 1800s, Baccarat began producing decorative perfume bottles of a non-commercial nature. Unusual stoppers and sculptured shapes became the focal point of many of the outstanding Baccarat flacons that followed. In 1907, the popularity of wedding the appeal of a perfume to the beauty of its bottle had captured the public's imagination to such an extent that Baccarat created a workshop devoted solely to the cutting of perfume bottles. This resulted in a host of beautiful scent bottles that rank among the finest ever produced . . . a tradition that continues today.

SAINT GOBAIN DESJONQUÈRE

Founded in 1665 as Saint Gobain, this early glassmaking facility was integrated into the illustrious Desjonquère operation in the 1950s. Saint Gobain Desjonquère stands along as the world's largest maker of perfume flacons, with a clientele list that includes a host of the best known and most popular icons in today's perfume industry.

The luminescent colorations and the minute faceting of its stopper make *Lumière* by Marchel Rochas both aptly named and worthy of "masterpiece" status. The 6.25" bottle is marked "SGD 4" (Saint Gobain Desjonqueres); the 5.25" bottle "HP 4" (Pochet Et Du Courval). Introduced in 1984, the bottle was designed by the Studio Rochas.

LUCIEN GAILLARD

A designer of Art Nouveau jewelry during the early 1900s, Gaillard's extraordinary talents did not escape the discerning eye of René Lalique, who became his mentor. Lalique subsequently encouraged Gaillard to utilize his jewelry-making artistry into the fashioning of perfume flacons. The results were spectacular, with Gaillard responsible for many outstandingly beautiful Art Nouveau style flacons used by French perfumeries of the day.

POCHET ET DU COURVAL

Le De Givenchy by Givenchy, with bottle manufactured by Pochet et du Courval, introduced in the early 1960s; shown here in 8" factice with 3" matching bottle of Givenchy's *Enterdit*, introduced in 1957.

One of the earliest bottlemakers in France was Pochet et du Courval, founded in 1623. Some three hundred years later the company converted solely to the production of perfume bottles (identified by the "HP" marking), with a long and continuing list of renowned clientele.

In four styles and sizes . . . *Bal à Versailles* by Jean Desprez. The factice measures 12" x 7.25". Marked "Made in France." Introduced in the early 1960s. With a bottle design by Pierre Dinand, the label features a reproduction of Fragonard's painting from the Sèvres museum. Bottles by Pochet et du Courval.

A clean, modern design featuring a bold Lucite top complemented by frosted center panel front and back and elegant black script, made for *First* de Van Cleef and Arpels. Bottle marked "HP, Made in France" (Pochet et du Courval). 4.75"

Billowing like an undulating headdress in a pharaoh's tomb, this frosted stopper caps a graceful 7" bottle of *Daniel de Fasson*. Marked "Made in France," the "HP 2" indicates the bottle was manufactured by Pochet et du Courval.

VERRERIES BROSSE

Founded in 1854 and originally devoted to the production of bottles of all kinds, Verreries Brosse recognized the market opportunities that emerged during the 1920s in the packaging of perfumes and, consequently, converted solely to the production of perfume flacons. Marked "VB" or "BR," some of the finest stoppered bottles available today come from this firm.

Settled regally on a marbleized base with brass plate for personalizing, this *Giorgio* factice is a towering tribute to the beauty of crystal, presented in a crisp yet sensuous design. Made in France by Brosse. 11.5 bottle, 3" stand.

J. VIARD

A sculptor renowned for his work during the 1920s, J. Viard had skills that were well suited to the design of fragrance bottles. Combining the influence of both the Art Nouveau and Art Deco periods, some bottles were signed "J. Viard," others "J. Villard."

THE BOTTLE BEAUTIFUL... PAST & PRESENT

Beautiful bottles filled with favorite scents are not only visual delights, but also serve to enhance the overall appeal of their contents. Glittering facets of glass, unusual modernistic shapes, bold or subdued colorations, whimsical figurals, and graceful stoppers all heighten the anticipation before the aroma sealed within fills the air.

Pictured here is a sampling of bottles, encompassing familiar "standards" that cannot be excluded from any "masterpiece" theme as well as rare and unusual bottles that command attention for their complex designs and eye appeal. Not presented solely because of current value or rarity, each of these commerical and non-commerical bottles is a stunning tribute to the skills of designers and glassmakers worldwide.

NON-COMMERCIAL BOTTLES

On the following pages are an assemblage of non-commercial fragrance bottles. From cut and pressed glass to porcelain, opaline, and brass, each has an exclusivity of style or design that elevates it to "masterpiece" status. Purchased to house the buyer's personal fragrance choices, their beauty has enhanced dressing tables, shelves, and countertops since scents were first concocted and recognized for their pleasure . . . and power!

Ambre De Nubie, Ramses, Paris (1922).

Sphinx, Dralle-Hamburg (1920s).

This rare bottle was designed by Heinrich Hoffman and made in Austria in the 1920s or 1930s, with the Hoffman intaglio butterfly marking. 8.75" high, the opaque black bottle sits in a sterling silver jeweled base decorated with faceted topaz-colored glass stones backed with faceted black glass faux gems. The feet of the base are topaz-colored glass. The neck of the bottle is encircled with a sterling silver band adorned with marcasites. The black opaque stopper is topped with a jeweled cap of sterling silver, marcasites, and black and topaz-colored faux gems. When the stopper is lifted from the bottle it reveals an opaque black dauber in the shape of a nude female. Photographs courtesy Donna Sims; photographer, Donna Sims.

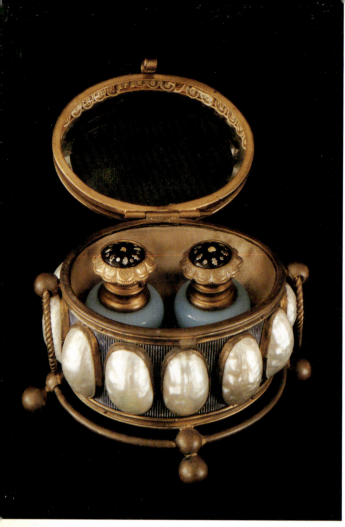

In a mother-of-pearl-encircled coffret, two decorative French opaline bottles, from the era of Napoleon III. Each bottle is 2-1/8". Coffret with beveled glass top measures 3.25" x 4.5". Courtesy Renee Gold

A blue opaline dresser set with gold Greek key designs, mid-1800s. Bottles 4.5"; powder jar 2.5". Courtesy Renee Gold

This opaque blue fragrance bottle measures 4", mid-1800s. Courtesy Renee Gold

White French opaline bottle, cased in spider-web, gold ormolu design. Hinged stopper. Nineteenth century. 2.75". Courtesy Renee Gold

White French opaline with gold decorated top and stopper, from the era of Napoleon III. 5.5". Courtesy Renee Gold

Encased in glass, four different architectural drawings surround this 6.75" x 4" blue opaline bottle of French origin, which is encaged in heavily-decorated golden scrollwork. Note figural at top. From the era of Napoleon III. Courtesy Renee Gold

French opaline bottle with floral cloisonné stopper and elaborate gold accents on equally decorative base. Mid-1800s. 4.75" x 3". Courtesy Renee Gold

Four French opaline bottles in blue, green, and white, all with ormolu trim and tops featuring Parisian architectural drawings encased in glass. From the era of Napoleon III. Each 2.25". Courtesy Renee Gold

Affixed permanently to its soapstone base, this charming presentation is French opaline with a small dish for trinkets and a dainty perfume bottle, all decorated with ormolu and a glass-encased architectural painting. From the era of Napoleon III. 5" x 4.5". Courtesy Renee Gold

Intended to be carried, worn via the attached chain, or admired as "laydowns" on the dressing table, these hinge-topped French opaline bottles are from the mid-1800s. The blue bottle stands 3" tall and has gold appliquéd designs; the round pink bottle is decorated with delicate floral enameling; the green bottle in front is similar to the popular barrel-shaped flacons but has a flattened back. Courtesy Renee Gold

Shown front and back, this turn-of-the-century fragrance bottle was designed to hang in madame's boudoir from its golden cord. It was purchased in Italy and traveled the ocean with its proud Victorian owner. Featuring brilliant colors and elaborate designs influenced by mythology, it is now a treasured family heirloom. 6.5".

Separated on both sides by velour-topped trinket boxes, four green opaline bottles fit into the side sections of this French *necessaires* box. The decorative container has a drop-front panel, and measures 12.75" x 5". Each gold-decorated bottle is 3.5" high. Circa mid-nineteenth century. Courtesy Renee Gold

In a glorious pale citrine with finite etchings, this heavy-based Bohemian scent bottle measures 7" x 3.5". Circa mid- to late 1800s. Courtesy Renee Gold

Czech bottle made of cameo glass.

Czech fragrance bottle.

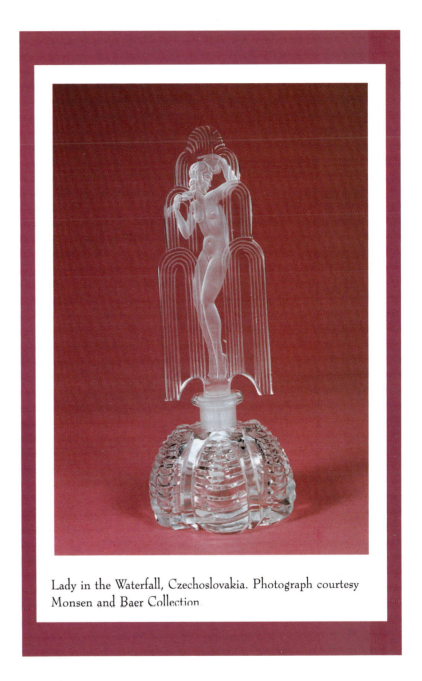

Lady in the Waterfall, Czechoslovakia. Photograph courtesy Monsen and Baer Collection

The Harem Dancer, Czechoslovakia. Photograph courtesy Monsen and Baer Perfume Bottle Auction.

Flower Basket, Czechoslovakia. Photograph courtesy Monsen and Baer Perfume Bottle Auction.

Butterfly Tiara in pink crystal, Czechoslovakia. Photograph courtesy Monsen and Baer Perfume Bottle Auction.

Art Deco nude dancer, Czechoslovakia. Photograph courtesy Monsen and Baer Perfume Bottle Auction.

Leda and the Swan in vaseline glass, by Hoffman, Czechoslovakia. Photograph courtesy Monsen and Baer Collection.

Malachite crystal dresser set, Czechoslovakia. Photograph courtesy Monsen and Baer Perfume Bottle Auction.

Steuben Gold Aurene bell-shaped bottle. Photograph courtesy Monsen and Baer Perfume Bottle Auction.

Signed "Czechoslovakia," this bottle features a cross-hatched design on the base, and a nude dancer and scarf on the dauber. Artist, Ivanhoe Gadpaille.

This urn-shaped bottle from the late nineteenth century graced a Victorian lady's dressing table. Of porcelain with gold leaf accents, it measures 9.5" x 5.5". The only maker's identification is a deeply indented "51" on the bottom.

Mold-blown pink Czechoslovakian bottle and stopper. Circa 1920. 5". Courtesy Jeannie Roberts

This cut-glass perfume bottle boasts a beautifully detailed sterling top. Circa late 1800s. 4.5". Courtesy Jeannie Roberts

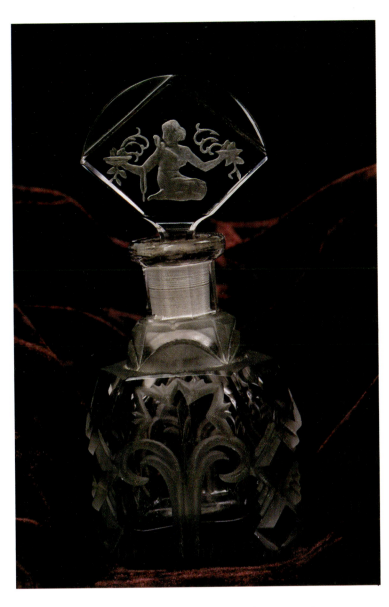

Czechoslovakian Art Deco perfume bottle. Strong design, beautiful lines, and a lovely intaglio of a kneeling woman accentuate the femininity of the piece. 4.75" x 2.25". Courtesy Jeannie Roberts

In a soft shade of violet, this perfume bottle has matching frosted intaglio, decorated base, and stopper. The bottom is acid-etched, "Made in Czechoslovakia." Courtesy Jeannie Roberts

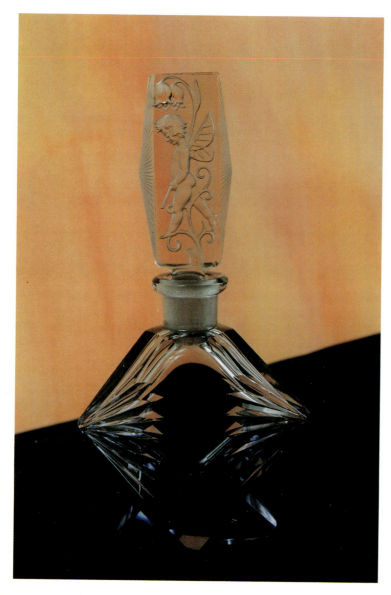

In royal purple and with an Art Nouveau influence, this finely detailed Czechoslovakian perfume features a giant stopper with faerie intaglio accented with lily of the valley. 6" x 3.5". Circa 1920s. Courtesy Jeannie Roberts

Art Nouveau sterling smelling salt, stamped "pat. 1898." 4.5" x 1". Courtesy Jeannie Roberts

Spectacular horn-shaped perfume bottle made of hand-cut crystal. Circa 1920s. 2.5" long with a 4"-wide stopper. Courtesy Jeannie Roberts

Dainty turn-of-the-century perfume with hinged opening. Courtesy Jeannie Roberts

Purple Czechoslovakian perfume with unusual stopper of frosted roses and faerie intaglio. The molded bottom features female dancers and a nude male piper. 4.75" x 2-1/2". Circa 1920s. Courtesy Jeannie Roberts

Side-bar atomizer made of heavily cased crystal; unsigned. 5".
Courtesy Renee Gold

In a Middle Eastern urn shape with brilliant red atomizer and
sparkling stones, this brass filigree beauty dates from the
1930s. 6.5". Courtesy Jeannie Roberts

Each of these cologne bottles, circa 1930, sport jeweled filigree holders; two have matching trays. The bottle with gold top sans tray is marked "Apollo." Each is 5" to 5.25" high and approximately 1.75" wide. Courtesy Jeannie Roberts

A highly-detailed 1930s brass filigree perfume is made even more regal by its purple jewels. 7" x 3.25". Courtesy Jeannie Roberts

Circa 1930s, brass filigree perfume with red jeweled accents and matching tasseled atomizer. 7". Courtesy Jeannie Roberts

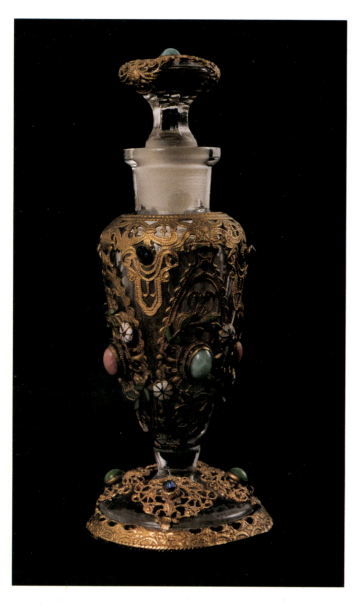

Czechoslovakian amber perfume with frosted high relief floral stopper. The decorative brass filigree is accented with a purple stone. 5" x 3". Circa 1920s. Courtesy Jeannie Roberts

This jeweled perfume bottle is adorned with lacy brass filigree and enameled flowers and leaves. Circa 1920s. 5.75". Courtesy Jeannie Roberts

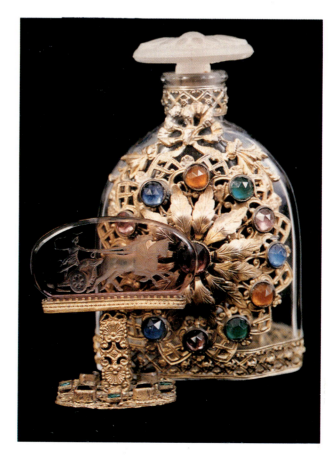

From the 1930s, a highly detailed brass filigree bottle, enhanced with colorful jeweled stones. 5" x 3". Courtesy Jeannie Roberts

Sporting its original atomizer, this handsome perfume bottle features red and blue jewels amid elaborate designs and filigree work. Circa 1930s. 6". Courtesy Jeannie Roberts

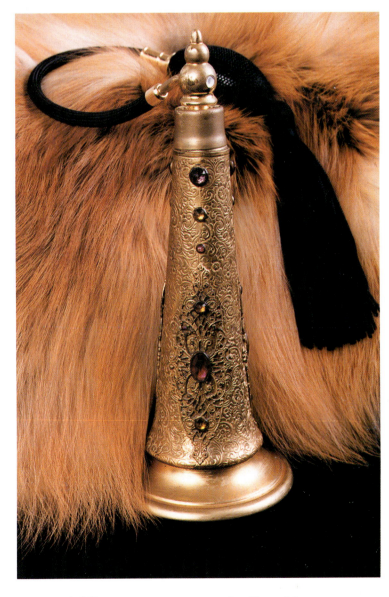

Jeweled like an Eastern potentate, this filigreed beauty is marked "Apollo" and dates from the 1930s. 7". Courtesy Jeannie Roberts

Circa 1920s, this graceful brass filigree perfume has a Middle Eastern flair and sumptuous jeweled adornments. 6". Courtesy Jeannie Roberts

From an Art Deco boudoir set. The perfume is 5.5" high; the powder jar is the same height and 5.5" in width. Courtesy Jeannie Roberts

Magnificent to behold! This pair of Venetian glass bottles rise 15.5" high, with glass-cased bottoms and white interiors. The regal floral stoppers have long daubers. Photograph courtesy Sharon and Howard Weatherly

A nineteenth-century sterling enameled perfume bottle with hinged top, hanging from a fleur-de-lis pin. French, of superior craftsmanship. Courtesy Jeannie Roberts

Elegant Bristol glass perfume bottle from the 1880s, with emerald green atomizer, gold leaf, and floral enameling. 4.5". Courtesy Jeannie Roberts

Richly-detailed with enameling, this contemporary atomizer is marked "1985-7181, Fellers." 4.5" diameter. Courtesy Renee Gold

By the famous Goebel company of Germany, a voluptuous black glass atomizer for madame's dressing table. Courtesy Renee Gold

Resembling some Lanvin and Babani designs, this perfume burner is unidentified. In popular use for centuries, a burner (and recipe in Edward IV's handwriting) were discovered after his untimely death in 1553 at age eighteen. By the end of that century, liquid perfume came into use, replacing the incense-type scents used previously, thus ushering in a plethora of perfume burners in many styles and materials in which liquid perfumes could be placed. By the nineteenth century, flameless burners came into use, enabling fragrances to continue to waft through the air long after the flame (and soot) had gone out, being controlled solely by the remaining oil. Pastille burners, often miniatures of buildings or toys, were popular with the "common folk." Produced by companies like Spode and Derby, they were charming replicas, some with removable parts and often with smoke escaping through the tiny chimney! Burner shown courtesy of Renee Gold.

Numbered and marked "Germany," this comical, charming bellhop atomizer is amazingly detailed (note his three-dimensional eyes!). 8.25". Courtesy Marilyn Kearney

Designed as an atomizer (originally attached to the pigtail), and patented in 1883 by J. G. Justin, this milk glass bottle has "Oriental" embossed at the base. Note his delicately flowered vest. 5.75" Though it was produced in large quantities in Germany and Bohemia, milk glass is generally acknowledged to have reached its peak under the aegis of English glassmaking operations. Courtesy Marilyn Kearney

Matching pair of heavily decorated, cut crystal dresser bottles, circa 1940s. 7.25". Courtesy Renee Gold

Elaborate Czechoslovakian cut glass bottle in a delicate shade of purple. Circa 1920s. 6". Courtesy Jeannie Roberts

Three heavy crystal, purse-size parfum sprays, marked "Vieux-Rouen, France." Each 3". Courtesy Renee Gold

This modernistic, spiral-topped crystal atomizer, measuring 3" x 2.75", is marked "Escale Bte SGDG, Marcel Franck, Made in France." Franck atomizers in this particular style were offered from 1936 until 1972. This example is most probably of the earlier vintage. Courtesy Renee Gold

Sleek 2.75" Art Deco-style atomizers for dressing table or purse, marked "Marcel Franck, Made in France." These are made of chrome, although others of similar design had different finishes, even snakeskin. This particular style was called "Le Weekend." Circa late 1940s. Courtesy Renee Gold

Contemporary perfume bottle with a luminescent design of fragile, delicately blowne glass. Marked "Egypt." 5.75". Courtesy Renee Gold

COMMERCIAL FLACONS

*"Offer a woman the best product you can make
and present it in a perfect container
(beautiful, simple, but in the best possible taste),
ask a reasonable price for it
and you will have a commercial proposition
such as the world has never seen."*
(Francôis Coty)[1]

Designed and marketed to house specific fragrances, commercial bottles (along with name recognition and overall packaging and advertising) play a major and understandably critical role in a perfume's popularity and financial success.

Every scent cannot "capture the senses" of every woman. What appeals to one is bound to be anathema to another, for fragrance is indeed very personal. However, individual preferences with regard to the contents do not detract from the artistic appeal of the bottle itself. Whether sold in large quantities to mass markets or in smaller numbers to a more exclusive clientele, appreciation of the beauty of a specific bottle can only enhance its ultimate collectibility.

Madhva by Fontanis

A souvenir of the 1893 Chicago World's Fair, this rare hot-air balloon perfume bottle was called the *Columbian Air Ship* and is filled with an unidentified fragrance. Marked "Philadelphia Novelty and Perfume Company," a patent date of May 24, 1892 is also identified. Note that the *Columbian Air Ship* designation is partially visible at the base of the bottle. From the Carole and Jim Fuller Collection. Photograph courtesy Donna Sims; photographer, Donna Sims.

The first fragrance created exclusively for a department store, John Wanamaker's *Queen Mary*, introduced in 1881, and shown here in two dynamic Victorian designs. The larger 8" bottle has an elaborate pyramid-style stopper and still contains some of the original "juice." It features an overlapping circular design above a row of fleur-de-lis. The smaller 6.75" bottle is of finely crackled glass with original Wanamaker price tag of $1.35 still attached to the bottom. Although inexpensive by today's standards, $1.35 would purchase an elaborate dinner for two at a fine turn-of-the century restaurant and, for the average worker, probably represented more than a full day's pay.

A Richard Hudnut classic. *Tout Mon Jardin* potpourri sachet, in a bottle style reflective of the Victorian ambiance so popular at the turn of the century. Introduced in 1914. 5"

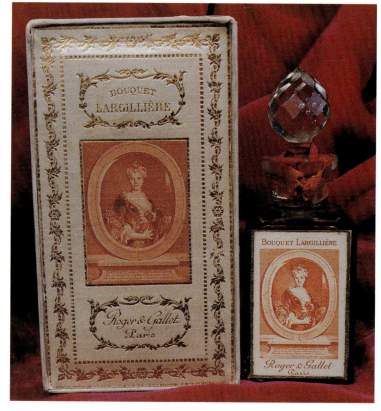

An unusual find, still in packing carton with embossed seal intact. As shown, the seal is also embossed into the box, with a gilt seal gracing the inside box cover. Named for a great beauty of late eighteenth century aristocracy, *Bouquet Largillière* is by Roger & Gallet; circa 1910. Courtesy Dennis Caron.

Etoile De Napoléon, elegantly presented by Viville, Paris. The accompanying advertisement is from a 1913 issue of *L'Illustration*. Courtesy Dennis Caron

One of Roger & Gallet's earliest fragrances, trademarked 1892 . . . *Vera-Violetta*. This presentation included its own blue leather case. Courtesy Dennis Caron

Stylishly in sync with the "hooked on angels" contingent, *Fleurs D Amour* by Roger & Gallet, Paris, featuring ethereal silver and gold label. The talc container has a deeply-grooved "R&G" in diamond design on the bottle's back. The fragrance bottle is 4.25" with multi-faceted stopper. Introduced in 1902.

From the parfumerie La Rose Dorée in Nice, a rare promotional giveaway that opens like two petals for *Roses D'Orsay* parfum, introduced around 1914. Back and front view shown.

Isabey's *Le Lys d'Isabey* ("The Isabey Lily"), by Dépinoix. Monsen and Baer Perfume Bottle Auction.

In a turn-of-the-century Victorian style, but with an ornate and colorful Oriental label, this bottle with frosted stopper still contains *Corylopsis* by Fantine. 5".

From a 1924 issue of *Century* magazine, a colorful advertisement for *Mon Boudoir,* introduced in 1905 by Houbigant.

Beautiful turn-of-the-century Art Nouveau engravings of perfume advertisements, hand-colored and attributable to Alphonse Mucha. Featured are *Muquet* by Coty, *Nenuphar* and *Bouton de Rose*.

In the popular style of 1920s and 1930s non-commercial dressing table bottles, this one was actually produced for a specific scent, *Kismet,* by Captiband Perfumes, Ltd., N.Y. 7.75". Courtesy Renee Gold

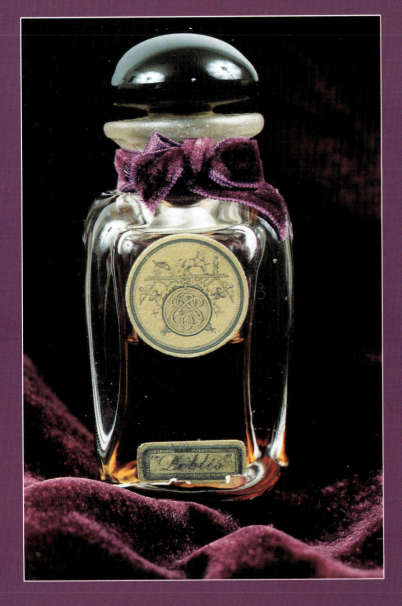
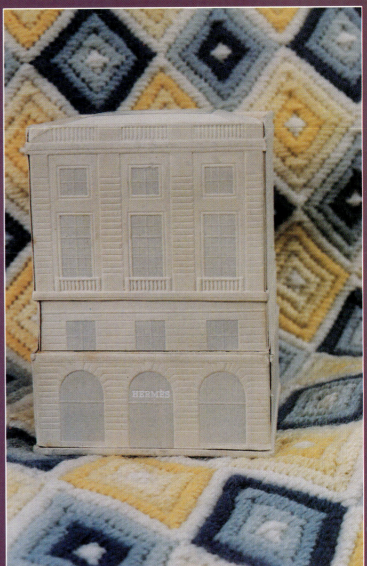

By Hermes, a crystal bottle of *Doblis*, presented in a velour cardboard replica of the Hermes building on Rue St. Honore in Paris, featuring a seal of the Greek god Hermes on outside of case. Circa 1960. Courtesy Dennis Caron

From the back covers of 1912-1914 issues of *Gazette du Bon Ton*, rare advertisements for Pinaud's *Pravia* and *Nebula*.

Ramses, Sidon, Paris (1920s).

With Art Nouveau decorative side panels, a faceted crystal stopper, and colorful label, this early twentieth-century bottle held *Pleasant Memories* by the French firm Vivi. Bottom marked with a diamond-shape centered with an "I". 6".

This magnificent bottle combines Art Nouveau designs in an Art Deco styling that features black-embossed figurals. The flacon held *Ambre De Delhi* by Babani. Marked "Babani, Deposé, Paris, France," the gold stopper has facets that glitter like a festive ballroom decoration. The sides are gold-striped, over clear, grey glass, and it measures 6.25" x 3.25". Strangely enough, the Babani company, located in Paris and headed by Maurice Babani, originally gained fame as fine-quality luxury shirt makers, and it was from this boutique setting that the somewhat unusual progression to fragrances occurred. Babani's shirt-making expertise attracted an exclusive clientele, including many from the Near and Far East, and possibly explains his fondness for exotic-sounding fragrances with Persian, Indian, and Oriental influences, such as *Ming, Daimo, Ligeia, Rose Gullistan, Afghani, Saigon, Fleurs d'Annam,* and *Yasmak*. The names did, however, occasionally revert to the French, with fragrances like *Oeillet*. All of these were introduced by Babani prior to 1922, with *Ambre De Delhi* following in 1927. Although Babani fragrances are noted for the lush designs and fine quality of their bottles, the name of the flacon manufacturer remains shrouded in mystery. Courtesy Marilyn Kearney

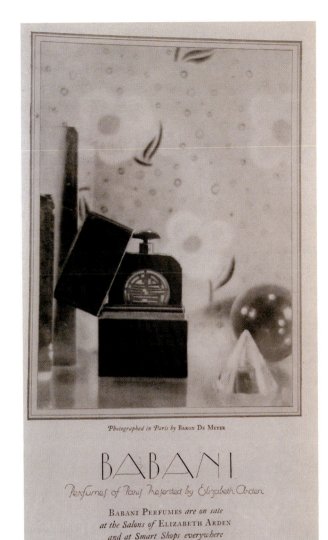

Photographed in Paris by Baron De Meyer

BABANI
Perfumes of Paris Presented by Elizabeth Arden

BABANI Perfumes are on sale
at the Salons of Elizabeth Arden
and at Smart Shops everywhere

Two advertisements for Babani fragrances. One, for *Ambre De Delhi* ("the breath of love"), is from the January 1918 issue of *Harper's Bazar*. The accompanying list shows the stores and spas in the United States where Babani fragrances were available, including all the Elizabeth Arden salons. The ad states that "Elizabeth Arden has chosen those created by Babani as the only perfumes worthy of being sold with her famous Venetian Toilet Preparations." The exclusive U.S. distributor was DeCameron Inc. The second advertisement, from a 1920 issue of *Harper's Bazar*, was photographed by Baron De Meyer, and is accompanied by a list of Babani fragrances. Note that prices ranged from $2.50 to $20, quite expensive for that time.

Babani Fragrances

MON AMIE ELIZABETH
$27.50

NANDITA
$20

EXTRAIT D'AMBRE GRIS
$18

GIARDINI
$12

AMBRE DE DELHI
$2.75 $7 $9 $12

LIGÉIA
$2.75 $7 $9.50 $10

MING
$2.75 $6.50 $9 $15

AFGHANI
$2.75 $7 $9 $9.50

CHYPRE
$2.75 $7 $9 $12.50

SOUSOUKI
$2.75 $6.50 $9 $12

JASMIN DE CORÉE
2.75 $6.50 $8.50 $9.50

YASMAK
$2.75 $7 $9.50 $12

Cardboard display for L.T. Piver, featuring *Volt, Fetiche,* and *Printanel.*

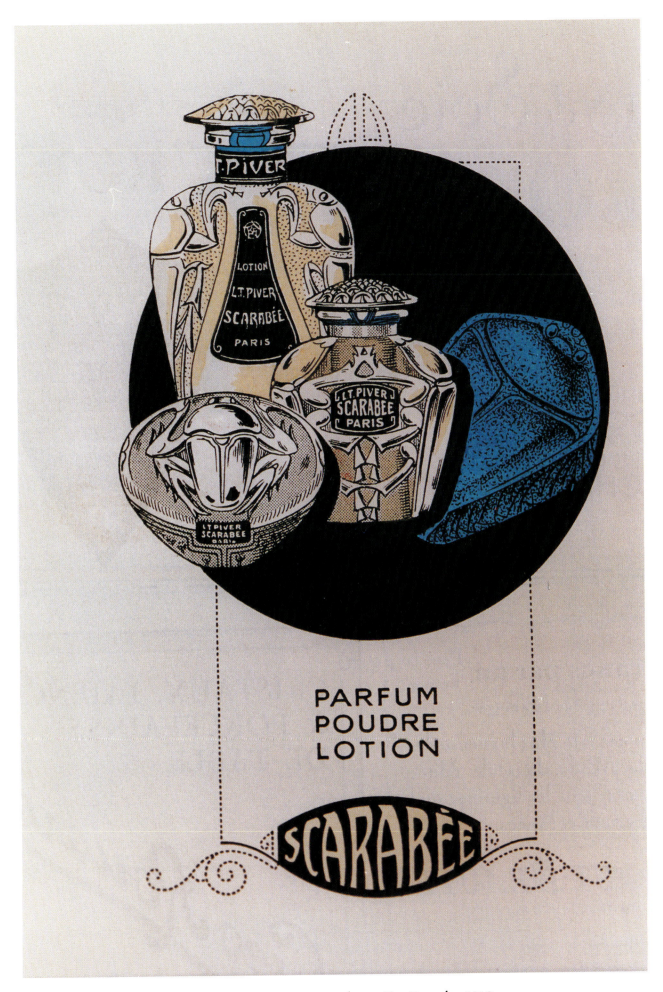

From the magazine *La Gazette du Bon Ton*, December 1913, a rare advertisement for *Scarabée* by L. T. Piver, especially remarkable since the *La Gazette du Bon Ton* featured very few perfume ads.

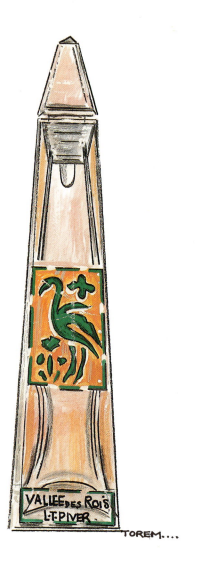

Vallée des Rois, L.T. Piver, Paris (1925).

Enigma, Lubin, Paris (1925).

The Andrew Jergens Company of Cincinnati, Ohio, introduced the fragrance *Ben Hur* in 1904. It was trademarked again in 1919, with this particular presentation most likely from the latter period.

Probably from circa 1915 or the early 1920s, this bottle housed *Parfum de La Parisienne* by R. Cerbelaud.

With the serene look of bygone days, this urn-shaped bottle, complete with the magnificent artistry of its box, held *Directoire* by Charles of the Ritz, circa 1945.

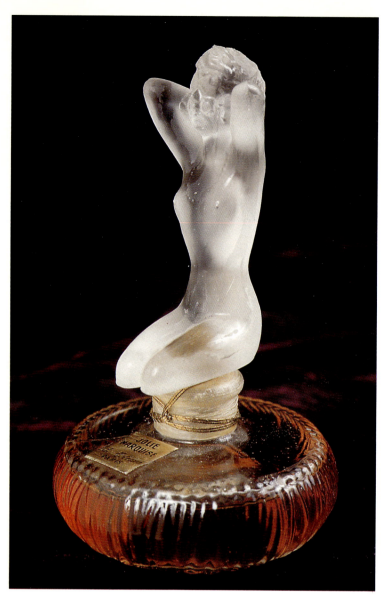 

On an exquisite base much like a tuffet, and complete with its mirrored presentation box, this nude figural was for *Jolie Marquis* by de Molinas, circa 1920. Modeled after Isadora Duncan, a similar bottle was later issued in the 1940s by Pierre Dune for *Sequoia,* and again in the 1980s by Isadora for *Isadora.*

For Mary Chess's *Souvenir D'Un Soir*, this nymph-like figural is part of a replica of the fountain St. Gaudens Pomona at the southeast corner of Central Park in New York City.

Also referred to as "The Secret of the Perle," the iridescent *La Perle d'Isabey* by the French house of Isabey was introduced in the early 1920s. An Isabey advertisement in a 1921 issue of *Harper's Bazar* also lists *Bleu de Chine; Lys; Ambré de Carthage; Sourire Fleuri;* and *Divertissement,* all of which were presented in flacons of similar style.

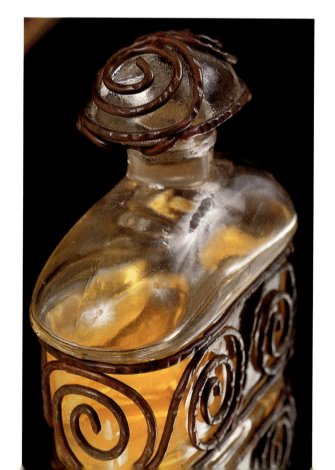

Le Balcon, a fragrance from the Rosine line of famed early twentieth century couturier Paul Poiret. Introduced in 1922.

In its plush coffret, *Wild Plum Blossom* by B. D. Baldwin Co. of Chicago. Originally offered in 1892, the fragrance was again trademarked in 1919. Photograph by Dorothy Torem; model, Michele Mathewson.

One of only a few Vionnet perfumes, the rare 'b' by couturier Madeleine Vionnet in a lift-top, pull-out velour box. The Deco-style bottle is 2.5". Probably from the 1920s-early 1930s period.

From the magazine *Art, Goût, Beaute*, rare 1921 advertisement for Ybry's *Femme De Paris*.

With a Yuletide theme, Lancôme's *La Nativité,* circa 1940s. Photograph courtesy Monsen and Baer Perfume Bottle Auction.

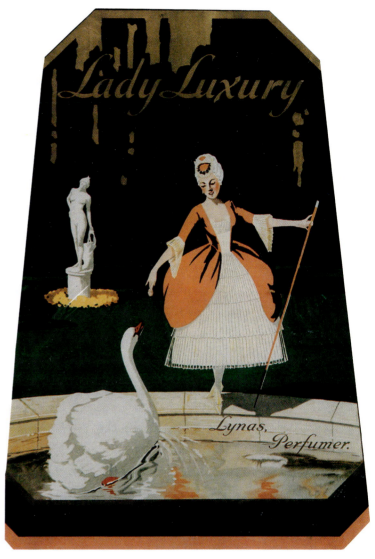

Stand-up display for *Lady Luxury* by Lynas.

Small but charming. This 2.5" opaque green perfume bottle is labeled "Vougay, Paris, France." The fragrance is *Sweet Pea Ambree.* Courtesy Jeannie Roberts

The elite of parfum whimsy, Vigny's *Le Golliwogg* needs no introduction. Of French origin, it was trademarked in 1919 and introduced in the United States in 1922. Derived from a colorful, turn-of-the-century character created by Florence Upton, it remains a collectible favorite. In 1895, Upton illustrated one of her British mother's children's books, and the Golliwogg was born! In Britain, this fantasy character achieved popularity—and a spin-off of products—much like that afforded Mickey Mouse in the U.S. With numerous spellings (Gollywog, Golliwog, and Golliwogg), Vigny chose to use *Le Golliwogg*. In both clear and frosted glass, Verreries Brosse created the bottle. Courtesy Dennis Caron. The *Le Golliwogg* advertisement dates from the 1920s.

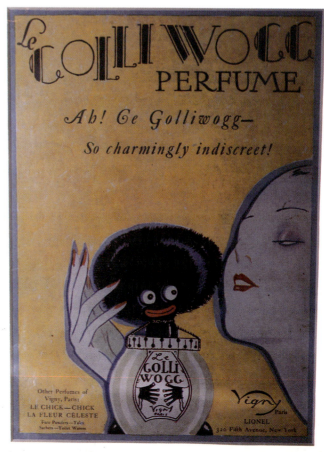

The elaborate frosted designs on the front and sides of this bottle for *Un Air Embaume* by Rigaud, featuring figurals and asps, are reflective of the Egyptian influence on the Art Deco movement, which was in its infancy when this fragrance was introduced in 1915. 4.5" x 3.5". Courtesy Renee Gold

Bohême, Arly, Paris. Of grey cut glass with frosted insets, this scent and flacon were introduced in the United States around 1915. Advertised as "Arly's Masterpiece," it sold for $4.00 (quite expensive for that time, equivalent to approximately half a week's salary for an average worker). 3" x 3.5". Courtesy Renee Gold

Molinard De Molinard, launched in 1980. Bottle marked "HP, Creation Lalique." The frosted overlay of female figurals is in the tradition of earlier designs by René Lalique, with the original style of this design created by him in 1929 for *Les Iscles d'Or*. 4" x 2-1/8"

With a delicate blue pineapple-design top in carved glass, this 3.25" heart-shaped bottle holds *Lov' Me* perfume, distributed by Blue Waltz (Joubert). Bottle marked "Made in U.S.A. '3'". Note pebbly design on heavy, frosted base. Circa 1930-1940s. Courtesy Renee Gold

In a straightforward design, the oversized gold stoppers and chess piece logos make these bottles of Mary Chess' *Gardenia* and *Yram* toilet waters appealing in their simplicity. Courtesy Renee Gold

Le Prestige by Moiret, Paris. Black glass, hobnail-style stopper, and overlapping designs combine in a beautifully constructed bottle. 4.25" x 3". Courtesy Marilyn Kearney

Mascarades by Cherigan, Paris. Charming black glass bottle featuring gold figural with hand and pursed lips silently signifying, "Shhh!" Marked "France." 4". Courtesy Marilyn Kearney

Photographed section by section, individual portions of a rare "perfume" scarf.

Grande Epoque
RENOIR

Vœu de Noel
CARON

Requête
WORTH

Magnificence
MOLYNEUX

Soir de Paris
BOURJOIS

Indiscret
LUCIEN LELONG

Rumeur
LANVIN

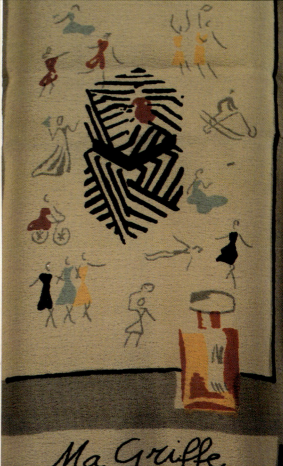

Ma Griffe
CARVEN

Ever After
PAQUIN

Bois des Iles
CHANEL

Marrakech
LANCOME

Plein Été
HOUBIGANT

Vol de Nuit
GUERLAIN

Normandie
JEAN PATOU

Réplique
RAPHAEL

Bandit
ROBERT PIGUET

Cœur-Joie
NINA RICCI

Antilope
WEIL

Cuir du Canada
DANA

Ulysse
CALIXTE

Cuir de Russie
L.T PIVER

Madras De Oriente by Myrugia of Barcelona, Spain, a fragrance launched in 1920. The 4.25" bottle features enameled flowers. The styling and appearance of the wooden coffret seems almost Egyptian in its design, lending an even more mysterious air to the Oriental name. Total height, 6". Courtesy Renee Gold

Circa 1993, a deluxe presentation of three re-issued Chanel classics, *Cuir De Russie*, *Gardenia* and *Bois Des Iles*. Courtesy Dennis Caron

The classic of classics! This highly effective, simple design, with slight variations, has served as repository for numerous Chanel scents, from *Chanel No. 5* to 1985's *Coco*. With bottle design by Jacques Helleu, the large flacon of *Coco* is 5.5" and contains 6.7 oz., the smaller is 3.5" with a 1.7 fl. oz capacity and a "VB 3" mark (Verreries Brosse). An almost generic term for perfume, "The name *Chanel No. 5* was such a quintessential French perfume that following the liberation of Paris in World War II, a line of American GIs over 300 yards long snaked down the avenue from Chanel's headquarters at 31 rue Cambon. There they waited patiently to purchase a treasured gift of *Chanel No. 5* for girlfriends, wives, and mothers back home."[2]

Le Roi Soleil by Schiaparelli, in a Baccarat crystal bottle designed by Salvador Dali, 1945

In a glass-domed red silk box, this innovative dressmaker's form held Schiaparelli's *Shocking*. Monsen and Baer Perfume Bottle Auction.

Marked "Bottle Schiaparelli, Made in France," although sometimes attributed to *Shocking*, it is more likely that this presentation was a special offering designed to hold a Schiaparelli fragrance of the purchaser's choice. The glass bottle and top are encased in a floral filigree design, each flower centered with a glittering red stone. Courtesy Marilyn Kearney

Opposite page:

This full-page Schiaparelli ad comprised the inside back cover of the December 1940 issue of *Stage* magazine.

Introduced as part of her "Display No. 2" sportswear collection in 1928, Schiaparelli's first perfume was *S.* Retailing for the then enormous sum of $21 an oz., it was a revolutionary "unisex" fragrance that was far ahead of its time! In 1934, S was updated and renamed *Schiaparelli.*

Early Schiaparelli perfumes were made in England by George Robert Parkinson, with Schiaparelli's ideas for fragrance packaging translated into designs and dummies by D. Guerycolas, an icon in the field of perfume design.

Souci was introduced in 1934. *Sleeping,* launched in 1938, featured a crystal Baccarat candlestick complete with taper and extinguisher. The name, however, lent itself to other merchandising interpretations, including drawing room scenes, and even canopied beds with two bottles tucked snugly under the covers!

Perhaps most recognizable, and certainly most renowned, was the bottle for *Shocking,* designed by Leonor Fini.

Schiaparelli's couturier background came to the fore in bottle design, with her brilliant idea of using the shape of a dressmaker's form, voluptuously presented in the style of the "naughty lady" of the silver screen, Mae West. Its manufacture at the Schiaparelli factory in Bois-Colombes was a tedious one, requiring the careful assemblage of twenty separate pieces, with thirty employees working full-time to make certain that all phases of the operation proceeded correctly. The advertising campaign added to the intriguing scenario, with Verté, one of the most inspired and renowned illustrators of the day, providing the drawings for this and other Schiaparelli fragrances (including the one shown here). To follow was Schiaparelli's *Zut,* which completed the second half of this parfum triumph, with the bottle now featuring the hips and legs of a female form.

With such imaginative marketing, it's no surprise that the fragrance side of Schiaparelli's business soon became its mainstay, for women who couldn't afford couture fashions by Schiaparelli could, nonetheless, revel in her scents!

Schiaparelli proves her expertise with masculine images. Here, a 7.5" bottle for *Snuff* Pour Homme, created exclusively for men, with chrome "smoking pipe" stopper. Introduced in 1940.

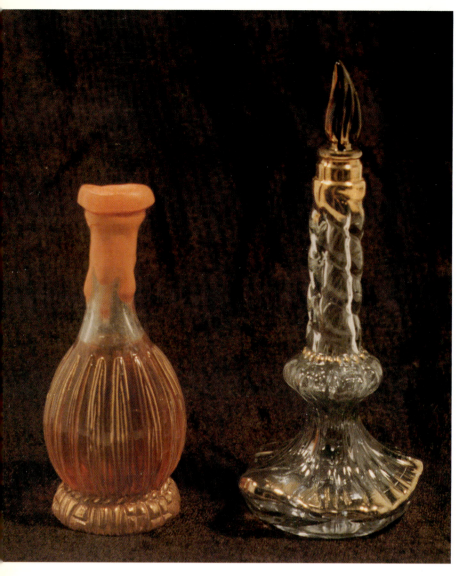

Two favorites by Schiaparelli. On the left, *Si,* introduced in 1957, here in a 4.5" bottle; on the right, a 6.5" *Sleeping,* introduced in 1937. Photograph courtesy Sharon and Howard Weatherly.

Richard Hudnut's *Three Flowers*, here in a 6.75" bottle. Fragrance originally introduced in 1915. Photograph courtesy Sharon and Howard Weatherly.

By Lady Grey, a Boston perfumery producing scents as early as 1891, this 3.5" presentation of *Raverie De Fleurs* is probably from the early 1900s. Photograph courtesy Sharon and Howard Weatherly.

By Revillon Parfums, Paris, presented as an inverted brandy snifter. 3". Photograph courtesy Sharon and Howard Weatherly.

In their own lucite case with lock and chain, three fragrances by Coty: *Meteor* introduced in 1949; *Larose,* and *Chypre,* an early Coty fragrance introduced around 1917. This presentation was probably from the 1950s. Each 4.5". Photograph courtesy Sharon and Howard Weatherly.

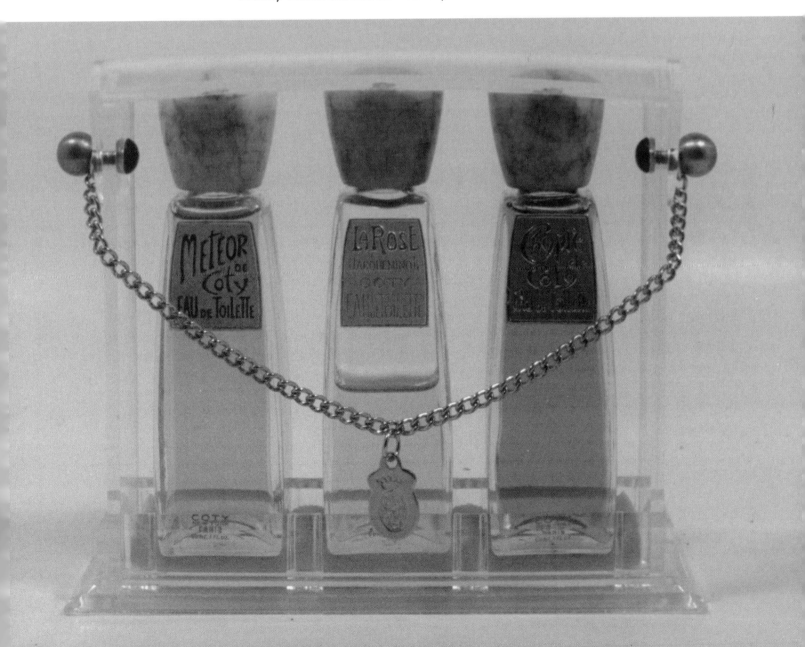

In mauve velour with ribboned top, a stately presentation for Christian Dior's *Diorissimo*, launched in 1956. The bottle measures 6". Photograph courtesy Sharon and Howard Weatherly.

This presentation case held three scents by Molinard, each measuring 3". Photograph courtesy Sharon and Howard Weatherly.

Jicky, one of Guerlain's earliest fragrances, introduced in 1889, endured for many decades thereafter. This presentation is in a 4" Baccarat bottle. Photograph courtesy Sharon and Howard Weatherly.

Jean Patou's *Moment Supreme*, with engraved and frosted initials on the stopper. 4". Photograph courtesy Sharon and Howard Weatherly.

With bold stoppers, two lovely Fabergé bottles for an unknown scent. The tallest is 6". Photograph courtesy Sharon and Howard Weatherly.

Circa 1920s-1930s, with a charming, feminine ambiance that reflects its Deco/Art Moderne origins. Although not identified, this stunning bottle was most likely designed by Jollivet for a fragrance aptly named *Lady*. The style is similar to other Jollivet designs for DeRaymond.

Replete with old favorites, a colorful double-page advertisement for Lentheric Parfumeur fragrances. *Vogue*, April 1939.

With scalloped stopper, a 6" flacon for *Spellbound* by Lynette. Circa 1943.

An ingenious presentation for the dressing table . . . each glass "grape" vial contains *Cyclamen* by Rochambeau.

On wings of eagles and touched with a regal air . . . gold, crown-topped bottle for *Nikki* by New York-based Orloff. Note eagles in profile flanking each side of the 4.5" x 4.75" bottle. Introduced in 1939.

Heavenly! D'Orsay's *Divine*. Photograph courtesy Monsen and Baer Perfume Bottle Auction.

Emeraude by Coty takes center stage in this blue silk presentation box with yellow mirrors. Photograph courtesy Monsen and Baer Collection.

La Soirée ("Evening Party") by Richard Hudnut, complete with its Moroccan leather box. Photograph courtesy Monsen and Baer Collection.

Looking every inch its name, *Crown Jewel* by Matchabelli sits regally in its velvet-lined box topped with white fur. Photograph courtesy Monsen and Baer Collection.

This bottle in heavy, stylized crystal is for *L'Ardente Nuit* by Corday. Although the frosted stopper is solid, it gives the illusion of an open design. Introduced in the late 1920s-1930 period. 5.25" x 3.5".

One of the most popular fragrance lines, reaching the peak of its popularity during the 1940s, '50s, and '60s, Prince Matchabelli offerings were readily available to the "average woman of average means." Their merchandising and design, noted for crown-shaped bottles and regal cross-shaped stoppers, place them in the "classic masterpiece" category. Shown are but a smattering of these lush designs—here, a towering 10" cork-stoppered bottle of pale green bath salts. The purple crown, bottom left, is of *Abano* skin perfume, the orange and green frosted bottles at right bottom are perfume creme sachets for *Wind Song* and *Stradivari*. The large bottle top right held *Wind Song*. At bottom center is green, gold-trimmed porcelain bottle marked "bottle made in France." Rising 8", the flacon with towering stopper at top left is labeled Bath Royale and contains bath oil in the *Verte* fragrance.

Probably part of a presentation set, this clip, featuring enamel and rhinestones, added incentive to purchase the accompanying Prince Matchabelli perfume. Courtesy Dennis Caron

Introduced in 1928, and probably purchased by more individuals than any other fragrance during its heyday (1930s into the 1940s), one of Boujour's vast array of presentations for *Evening in Paris*. Enveloped in the aura of "French perfume" and minus prohibitive price tags, it immediately captured the fancy of women of modest means in search of a morale boost during the Great Depression and World War II.

Evening in Paris by Bourjois takes on a particularly elegant air with its frosted stopper and silver, star-shaped box. Photograph courtesy Monsen and Baer Perfume Bottle Auction.

Scents of the times ... from the pages of *Stage* magazine, December 1940.

In the box and out . . . couturier Hattie Carnegie's first scent, aptly named *Hattie Carnegie* and launched in 1928. The gold decorated glass bottle with gold crown stopper is 3" x 3" and marked "Made in France." The box measures 3.75" x 3.5". Courtesy Marilyn Kearney

Introduced in 1944, a 22 carat gold-washed figural for Hattie Carnegie's *49*. The bottle was by Wheaton.

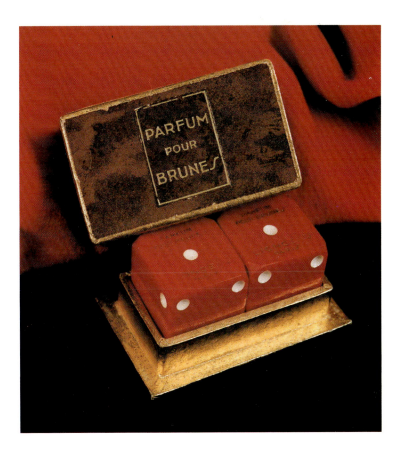

From the 1930s, *Parfum Pour Brunes* by Lionceau. With cherry red Bakelite dice, these are the most desirable of the available colors, the others being green and ivory. Courtesy Dennis Caron

Like an oversized ring box, this brilliant presentation opens to reveal *Grilou* by Jacques Griffe, Paris, amid luxurious grey satin. Flat-stoppered bottle marked "Made in France." 1.75" x 1.5". Courtesy Marilyn Kearney

Giant cardboard display for *Baccara* by L. T. Piver, introduced in 1959.

From Bertelli, an old Italian perfumer, this beautiful presentation of *Ebbrezza Marina* was issued circa 1950, and features an enormous dolphin in bas relief, along with a seashell and scallop motif on the box and label. Courtesy Dennis Caron

A familiar classic that cannot be overlooked in any display of outstanding designs, *Shalimar* by Guerlain needs no introduction, for it has captured the attention of women since the days of the 1920s flapper. The 5.75" x 4" flacon pictured here has its own violet-lined presentation box.

A gift of love . . . Nettie Rosenstein's *Odalisque*, introduced in 1946, in a giant 5.25 x 3.5" bottle, monogrammed with the recipient's initials. Bottle marked "Made in Italy." Note the flat-topped, frosted stopper, deeply etched "NR." The companion bottle measures 2" and held Rosenstein's *Fleurs d'Elle*, introduced in 1961.

Gemey by Richard Hudnut. Introduced in 1923, this fragrance remained a popular favorite, especially during the 1950s. 6.75". Photograph courtesy Sharon and Howard Weatherly.

Nestled in coral velvet, *Nueva Maja* by Myrugia, España. The gold-labeled crystal bottle measures 2.5". With its fiery colors and sultry image, the box alone is a masterpiece of design.

Le Jade by Roger & Gallet. Colorful, satin-lined box with floral, frosted-stoppered bottle. 3.5" x 2.5". Courtesy Marilyn Kearney

Milord by D'Orsay. Complete with top hat, an imposing gentleman in black decorates the lid of this quilted white box. Banded with ribbon, a complementary cameo-style figure adorns the frosted stopper. Box 2.25" x 3.25"; bottle 1.75" x 2.25". Courtesy Marilyn Kearney

D'Orsay's *LeDandy*. The gold-labeled, black glass bottle fits snugly into its complementary, velour-lined powder-box style container. Box 4.5" x 2"; bottle 3.5" x 2.75". Courtesy Marilyn Kearney

Guerlain's *Chamade,* launched in 1969. Measuring 5", it has a frosted stopper and gold embossed medallion. Marked "Guerlain Paris, Bottle made in France."

This renowned Marc Lalique design of the dove-topped bottle for Nina Ricci's *L'air du Temps* measures 3" and is complete with box.

For Coty's *Paris*, this advertisement graced the entire back cover of the December 1940 issue of *Stage* magazine.

Fragrance advertisements discovered in a German magazine from the World War II era.

This full-page ad for Corday's *Jet* graced the inside front cover of the December 1940 issue of *Stage* magazine.

Bal A Versailles, Jean Desprez, Paris (1969).

Of current vintage, this charming opaque blue bottle with three-dimensional red stopper was designed for *Lou Lou* by Cacharel, Paris. 3.75". Courtesy Renee Gold

Continuing in the Lalique tradition, Nina Ricci's *Nina*, introduced in 1987. With frosted glass in a deeply faceted, pleated design, the bottle measures 4.75" and is marked "Nina Ricci, Paris . . . Lalique, Made in France."

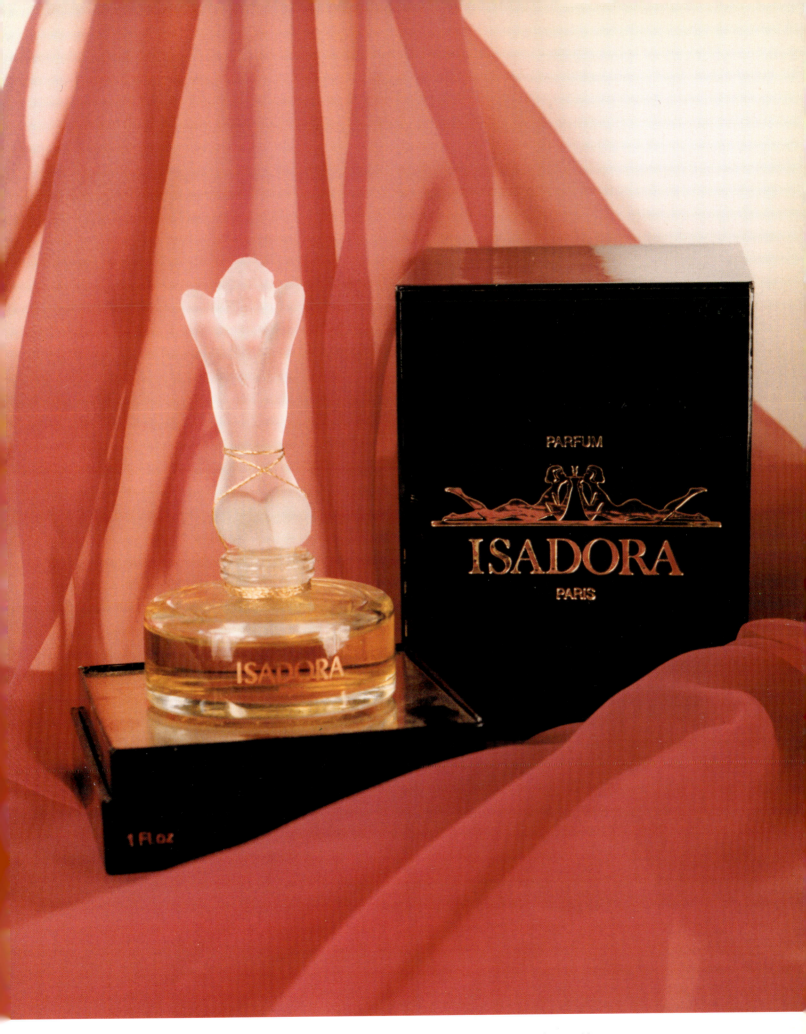

Measuring 4.5" and with its original packaging, the Parisian *Isadora*, with its gold-entwined, frosted nude figural stopper. Bottle marked "Isadora, 1979, Bottle made in France."

Of current vintage but reminiscent of Art Nouveau's halcyon days, this frosted 5.25" bottle of *Sirène* by France's Vicki Thiel features cavorting nudes encircling its circumference. A mini of similar design is in the forefront.

Head over Heels by Ultima II. Sure to garner attention, this deliciously "naughty" 7" presentation is a masterpiece of design ingenuity.

By Fabergé, the introductory packaging for a contemporary fragrance, *Joyau*. Launched in France, the bottle's Fabergé-like, egg-shaped opaque top conceals barely discernible sculptures with the futuristic look of frosty glaciers.

In a dynamic, heavy-walled design with sleek, modern stoppers, *Osé* by Guy Laroche, introduced in 1977. The largest is 3" x 2.5". Courtesy Renee Gold

Paloma Picasso in ovoid-shaped, sleek design, revealing fragrance at core. 4" x 2"

An innovative design. When removed, this surrealistic nude for *Sculptura* by Jovan reveals the frosted bottle's atomizer, which fits snugly inside the composition black base. 7.5" overall.

Ma Griffe Vapoisateur by Carven. Note contemporary, interlocking spirals on Lucite top. Made in France, the fragrance was launched in 1945. 6". Courtesy Renee Gold

Oscar de la Renta's *Volupté* in 2.75" and mini sizes. The emerald green, gold-rimmed stopper tastefully tops a simple yet effective bottle. Marked "Made in France."

Calvin Klein's signature bottle for *Obsession*. A masterful design, with its ovoid shape, three-layered composition stopper, and unusual brown colorations. 4.25" wide x 2.5"

In the style of a Victorian "laydown" but of current vintage, Ralph Lauren's *Lauren*. 4.5" Bottles for Ralph Lauren are produced by Cosmair. Courtesy Renee Gold

By Krizia, *Krazy Krizia*. Of current vintage, the sleek, contemporary top effectively complements the curves of the bottle's base.

With a sleek bottle and modernistic packaging to match, couturier Versace's *Gianni Versace*. Bottle designed by Alain de Mourgues and marked "HP 8" (Pochet et du Courval). Introduced in 1982.

By the Italian couturier and with a modernistic frosted top resembling an unfurling banner, this 3.75" x 3" award-winning bottle is for *Romeo Gigli*. Its frosted top varies from that of the accompanying mini with contrasting grey stopper.

THE MINI

"Good things come in small packages."

A coterie of perfume bottle collectors concentrate solely on the "mini." These bottles, tiny extensions of their larger counterparts, have a special charm that sets them apart. As a group, be it ten or hundreds, they make a glittering statement in a modest amount of space. Originally offered individually or as part of "trial size" combos, these tiny treasures stand alone or in groups as mini-masterpieces.

A set of three current Lalique miniatures designed by Marie-Claude Lalique, each featuring *La Parfum Lalique*. Courtesy Dennis Caron

Art Deco purse bottle with jeweled filigree and enamel work. 1" x .75". Courtesy Jeannie Roberts

1930s purse bottle with lacy brass filigree and red jewels. 1.5". Courtesy Jeannie Roberts

This purse bottle from the 1930s is encased in an elaborate filigree cage. 1.25". Courtesy Jeannie Roberts

159

Circa 1930s, footed purse bottle with filigree ornamentation and purple jewels. Courtesy Jeannie Roberts

Shaped like a tiny inkwell, this purse bottle with openwork filigree and blue jeweling has an added bonus . . . a band of four-leaf clovers encircling the cap! Circa 1930. 1.5". Courtesy Jeannie Roberts

This purse bottle, circa 1930, has large purple jewels, enamel work, and elaborate filigree. Courtesy Jeannie Roberts

Mini magic . . . Circa 1930, this clear purse bottle has opaque green flowers in molded relief set in brass filigree. During this time period, purse bottles were generally purchased to hold a dram of the buyer's favorite perfume. Courtesy Jeannie Roberts

Victorian sterling silver, enameled scent container to be worn around the neck. Courtesy Renee Gold

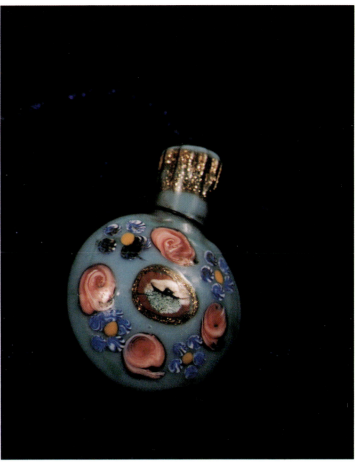

Miniature hand-blown Venetian glass perfume bottle with a rare center motif depicting a gondola. Circa 1900. 1.75". Courtesy Jeannie Roberts

Of earlier vintage than purse bottles, this tiny turn-of-the-century brass perfume bottle has rows of jewels and a colorful enameled center. 1.5" x 1". Courtesy Jeannie Roberts

This charming gold painted miniature of heavy glass was designed to contain the buyer's perfume of choice. Unsigned, it measures 2.5". Courtesy Renee Gold

This fashionable lady tops a mini parfum . . . and her head with a "watermelon" chapeau! Circa 1925. 2". Courtesy Jeannie Roberts

Caron's *Le Narcisse Noir* in golden purse container. 3".
Courtesy Renee Gold

In its mini Lucite case, Givenchy's *L'Interdit*, introduced in 1957; in the center is *Sortilege* launched by Le Galion in 1937, marked "Made in France, MCT, Inc."; and to the right, *Chypre*, introduced in the 1930s and distributed by Deltah. Courtesy Renee Gold

Typical of bottles from the late 1920s-1930s period, and charming for their simplicity and labels, this mini duo is by Ronni Perfumes Inc. One held *Lily of the Valley*, the other *Rare Orchid*. Contents .25 oz. Courtesy Renee Gold

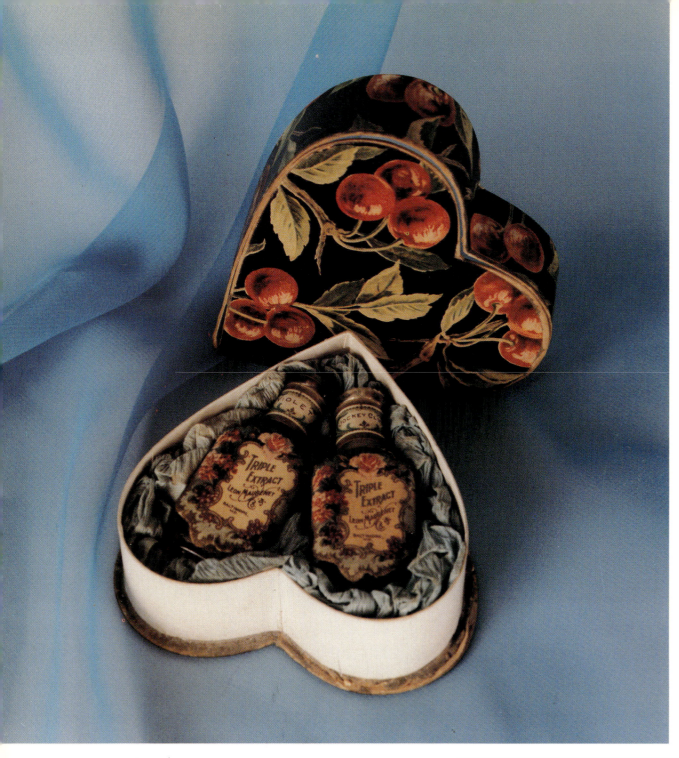

In an eye-appealing, heart-shaped box covered with cherries, tiny twins . . . *Violet* and *Jockey Club* Triple Extracts by Leon Maugenet, Baltimore. Cork-stoppered, with colorful floral labels. Box 3.5: bottles 2.5". Courtesy Marilyn Kearney

The interest here lies not in the simple style of the bottle but in Myrugia's colorful label of brilliant red and yellow for this miniature of *Blason*. Courtesy Renee Gold

A mini of Harriet Hubbard Ayer's *Pink Clover.* Introduced in 1938. Courtesy Dennis Caron

By Corday, *Voyage a Paris,* an exceptionally rare miniature replica from the 1930s. Courtesy Dennis Caron

A progression of three charming miniatures: on the right, a decorative, frosted bottle for Coty's enduring *Emeraude*, introduced in 1923; on the left, *Balalaika* by Lucien Lelong, introduced in 1939; and in the center 1948's *My Love* by Elizabeth Arden. Courtesy Renee Gold

French opaline miniature with hinged top; circa mid-nineteenth century, it measures 1.75". Courtesy Renee Gold

A miniature at its delicate best... the crystal bottle has gold floral enameling and a gold stopper and contained an unidentified fragrance by Harriet Hubbard Ayer.

Crepe de Chine by Millot, delightfully packed in Holiday style, with the bottle suspended in the middle of a clear plastic Christmas ball surrounded by red sequins and gold glitter. A gold hang tag and red bow complete the festive presentation. 3 cm. Photograph courtesy Arielle Hart

Richard Hudnut's *Le Début Vert,* complete with box. Photograph courtesy Monsen and Baer Collection.

In its gold box, *Le Pois de Senteur* ("Sweet Pea") by Renaud. Photograph courtesy Monsen and Baer Perfume Bottle Auction.

A colorful presentation . . . with red, cream, and dark blue accents, *Dress Parade* by Solon Palmer. 4 cm. Photograph courtesy Arielle Hart

The French maid . . . *Oh la la* by Ciro. The saucy black suede apron covering the bottle, the red bow accent, and the garter on the box makes this mini especially charming. Marked "Purse size." 5.4 cm. Photograph courtesy Arielle Hart

Ready for the masked ball . . . *Savoir Faire* by Dorothy Gray. The mask is stenciled on the bottle in black and gold. 4 cm. Photograph courtesy Arielle Hart

Asuma by Coty . . . Replica bottle of frosted glass encircled by molded flowers; ground glass stopper, seal intact. 3.8 cm. Photograph courtesy Arielle Hart

Repartee by Lentheric. This clear glass replica bottle has a knotted cord molded in the glass. The gold label wraps around the bottle, with "Repartee" on one side and "Lentheric" on the other. 4.3 cm. Photograph courtesy Arielle Hart

The swirling lines of the bottle are complemented by the pleated jabot design on the box. This striking presentation was for Lucien Lelong's *Jabot*. 4.5 cm. Photograph courtesy Arielle Hart

An innovative presentation for *Flair* by Yardley. In an unusual shape, this replica bottle is of clear glass with green composition screwtop. Shaped like a matchbook, the box appropriately reads, "Strike a New Note." 2.4 cm. Photograph courtesy Arielle Hart

An interesting dual-bottle concept by Helena Rubenstein, one marked *Town,* with a decorative skyscraper, the other *Country,* with a pastoral setting. (3.7 cm) Photograph courtesy Arielle Hart

Shaped like a leaf, two versions of Schiaparelli's *Succès Fou* are pictured, one with a green label with gold lettering, the other in the reverse. 3.6 cm. Photograph courtesy Arielle Hart

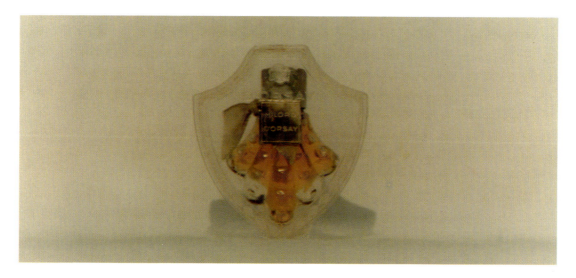

Milord by D'Orsay . . . Clear, shell-shaped laydown bottle with silver top, decorated with a gold hangtag and pale green ribbon tied at neck. The bottle sits in a clear hard plastic shield-shaped box that has "D'Orsay—Paris—France" molded in the plastic. 3.8 cm. Photograph courtesy Arielle Hart

Black Rose by the British company Goya. With base and top of deep red composition and title stenciled in dark red, this is a sultry presentation with a Latin flair. 4.2 cm. Photograph courtesy Arielle Hart

Kiku gold-stoppered parfum by Fabergé, with company name and scent name encircling the base in gold letters. .25 oz., 1.75". Courtesy Renee Gold

Double duty . . . a perfume flacon/brooch encrusted with faux amethysts.

This 3.5" diameter velour ball with crown crest holds a surprise . . . three miniatures (one dram each) of *Katherine the Great*, *Ave Maria*, and *Duchess of York* by Matchabelli. Courtesy Marilyn Kearney

Designed as a Jack-in-the-Box, this *Shocking* set by Schiaparelli contains three miniatures. Photograph courtesy Monsen and Baer Perfume Bottle Auction.

This Schiaparelli *Shocking* mini dressmaker bottle is particularly appealing for its all-glass design, including the tiny bulbous stopper. Issued in 1939.

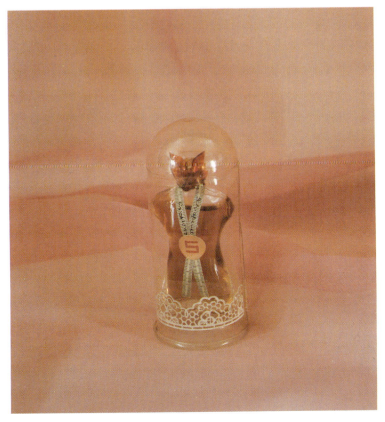

With a festive red bow, another mini dressmaker *Shocking* by Schiaparelli, this time encased in a 2.5" celluloid container. The bottle measure 1-5/8". Courtesy Marilyn Kearney

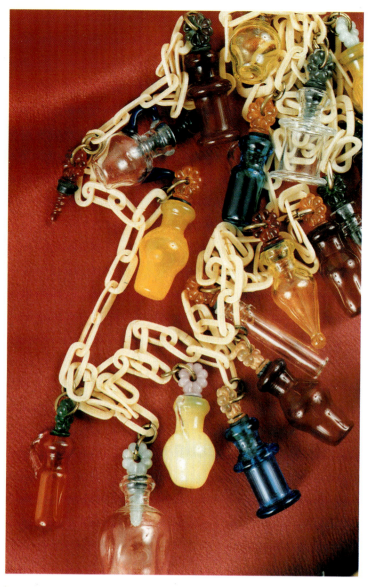

Whimsical necklace embellished with twenty multicolored, hand-blow glass miniature perfume bottles with screw tops. Circa 1920s. Courtesy Jeannie Roberts

A Concentrated Perfume by Lucretia Vanderbilt in a cylindrical trial-size case. The striped metallic holder contains a 1.75" bottle with frosted stopper and silver label. The case, with butterfly logo, is 2". Courtesy Marilyn Kearney

A rarely seen boxed set of ten 2ml mini flacons from Fragonard, France. The fragrances represented are *Fragonard, Oui Madame, Murmure, Natouna, Mazurka, Reve De Grasse, RendeVous, Reve Indien, Emilie,* and *Caresse.* The bottom of every bottle is marked "500," with the boxed sequence of each (1, 2, 3, etc.) underneath. Shown to the left is a *Magie Noire* mini by Lancome.

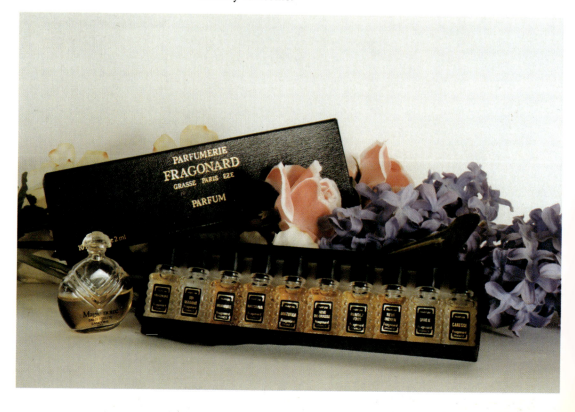

Gala Nights by Bouton, N.Y. With green Bakelite top, this mid-twentieth century miniature is 1.5" and rests in its green, faux leather box. Courtesy Renee Gold

Two minis by Park & Tilford flank their "big sister." On the left is *Desire*, introduced in 1957, on the right, *No. 3*, introduced in 1931. The 3.75" bottle in center held Park & Tilford's 1947 scent, *High Heels*. Each miniature is 1.5" with a contents of .85 dram. Courtesy Renee Gold

Holding .35 oz., a gold-topped *Evening in Paris* by Bourjois. 2.25". Courtesy Marilyn Kearney

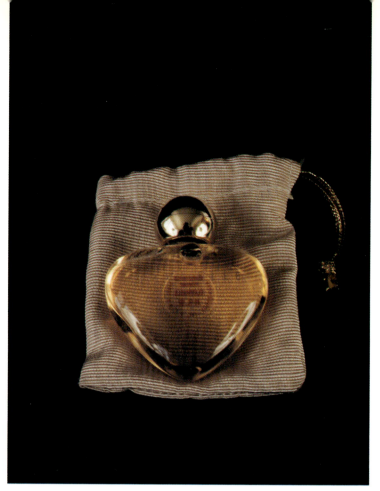

Pave Elle heart-shaped mini in moiré drawstring case, part of the Heart Strings series by Avon.

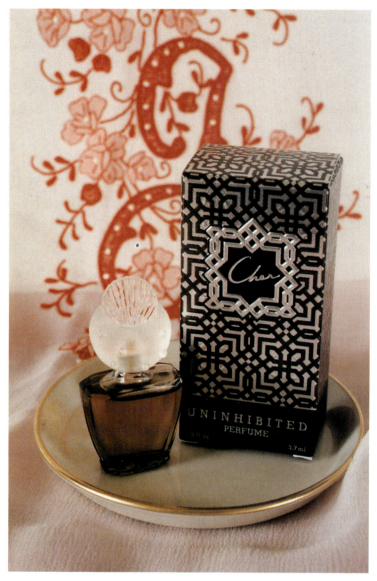

Exhibiting all the glamour of its colorful namesake, *Uninhibited* by Cher. Mini size with box.

Who else but the master of the surreal could have made this? Here is his own perfume miniature, *Salvador Dali,* in the shape of black lips, complete with mystical Dali design on the box. Courtesy Renee Gold

Red hot... *Samsara* miniature by Guerlain.

For the gentlemen... Ralph Lauren's chrome-topped *Monogram*.

Ingeniously designed, the fragrant center is framed by a spherical, modernistic black rim. Created to hold *Paloma Picasso*, this is a design triumph in any size.

Couturier Christian Lacroix's *C'est la vie!* (.34 oz.).

Flat stopper in same unusual design as its larger counterpart, *Trésor* by Lancôme.

In midnight blue and emerald green, a trio of colorful miniatures by world-renowned couturiers . . . left, *Ungaro*, center *Volupté* by Oscar de la Renta, and at right, Karl Lagerfeld's *Sun Moon Stars*.

Floral delights . . . *Chloé* by Karl Lagerfeld and *Cabotine* by Gres.

Bal à Versailles by Jean Desprez and Caron's *Nocturnes*.

The mighty duo . . . *White Diamonds* and *Elizabeth Taylor's Passion*.

This bathing beauty is a miniature delight . . . *Isadora* by Isadora, Paris. 2"

SOLID SCENTS

Until the advent of distillation processes in the seventeenth century, crude solid perfumes, ointments, and oils were the only types of scents in use (although fragrant waters, like lavender water, appeared in the middle of the twelfth century).

The history of solid perfumes is largely rooted in religion. The apple solid, one of the most popular shapes, was derived from the early practice of rolling melted castoreum into a ball-like shape by hand. Most popular from the Middle Ages onward, this ball was then hung from the neck or carried by hand, and was frequently attached to rosary beads. This form was also significant in the East; "In eastern culture the apple was a symbol of eternal life, of the Godhead and of power and strength."[1] Egg-shaped pomanders were also common, as were those fashioned in the shape of fish, both with religious connotations. From the mid-seventeenth century on, smelling boxes were popular, with the heart-shaped style and fish symbols becoming particular favorites. Thus, the smelling box served as a transitional vessel between the pomanders of old and the scent bottles of the eighteenth century. Vinagrettes, which were the flacons of choice during the early periods of liquid perfumes, were also popular for a very short time from the late eighteenth century until around 1850. In a vinagrette, "the container is provided with a well fitting lid and inside, under a removable grille, is a sponge soaked in the desired scent . . . In most vinagrettes the inside is lined with gold to avoid corrosion and undesirable smell caused by chemical reaction between metal and content."[2]

Solid scents of the twentieth century generally served as adjuncts to popular fragrances of the day. For dressing table, purse, and pocket—or even to hang 'round the neck or pin to a frock—they enjoyed particular commercial popularity at mid-century, and were often fashioned in shapes and styles that had been used for the same purpose centuries earlier. In addition to the eggs, apples, and fish were other fanciful designs, some encrusted with stones and resembling a piece of eye-catching jewelry, others fashioned like whimsical shapes from nature. Highly collectible, they represent yet another treasure in the vast array of perfumed collectibles.

Three jeweled and enameled eggs in "Fabergé style" solid perfumes. An Estee Lauder 1994 Christmas presentation. Courtesy Dennis Caron

For the sultry *Tabu*, introduced in 1932, Dana's solid perfume, circa 1960s, features a golden medallion with the company logo. Courtesy Dennis Caron

Set in dark blue enamel, the golden crown lends a regal air to Princess Marcella Borghese's *Fiama*. The top opens to reveal tiny wells of solid perfume. Courtesy Dennis Caron

For Revlon's *Ciara*, circa 1950s . . . an enameled watch case of solid perfume. Courtesy Dennis Caron

The music room . . . delightful gold figural solids, all by Avon. Photograph courtesy Sharon and Howard Weatherly

A chickadee and a silver apple, both unmarked, hold solid perfumes. Photograph courtesy Sharon and Howard Weatherly

To hold solid perfumes, the pearl- and gem-encrusted egg at left and the compact-style container with orange stones on the right are both unmarked; the heart-shaped container with filigree and pink stones is by Schiaparelli. Photograph courtesy Sharon and Howard Weatherly

Cameo delights! On left, a stunning rendition by Estee Lauder; the filigree, diamond-shaped one below is by Avon; the oval compact-style container and the necklace were by Max Factor. Photograph courtesy Sharon and Howard Weatherly

From faux pillboxes to necklaces, all held solid perfumes: top left, the container is by Florenza; top center for an Estee Lauder fragrance; the necklace, top right is unmarked; the two at bottom are by Helena Rubenstein. Photograph courtesy Sharon and Howard Weatherly

An open and shut case . . . with no maker's mark, this 2.25" diameter Bakelite beauty held a solid, unidentified fragrance.

Two solid perfumes by Max Factor, both featuring marvelous marbled eggs, circa 1960s. The basket is of *Hypnotique*, the bird's nest was for *Spring Song*. Courtesy Dennis Caron

ADVERTISING FANS

"Women are Armed with Fans, and Men with Swords"
("Ladies Gallery," February/March 1995)

Fans scented with fragrance date to the French court of the 1600s. Steeped in coquetry, they remained popular into the twentieth century, reaching their apex during Art Deco's heyday. During that period, scented advertising fans touted everything from night club promotions to the wearability of silk stockings. The fragrance that wafted through the air with each flutter of these fans must surely be credited as an early example of subliminal advertising.

Cort Theatre advertising fan dated August 26, 1914 for *Desti* perfume. Note the thorny-stemmed rose!

Charming figurals in gossamer pastels adorn this advertising fan for L. T. Piver's parfum *Oreade* ("nymphs"). The bottom photograph shows the opposite side.

Advertising fan for Palomeras and Pucci Ltd., with a list of perfumes available from their French Bazaar.

From Galeries Lafayette, this fan features an elegant lady . . . while its opposite side touts both silk hosiery and *M'Lati* parfum. Circa 1924.

THE FACTICE & DISPLAY BOTTLE

As the saying goes, "Presentation is everything." So are first impressions. Indeed, a gaily wrapped package is often admired and appreciated long before its contents are disclosed. It is this initial contact that frequently lies at the heart of the success or failure of a given product.

The highly competitive fragrance industry is ever-mindful of the link between the eye and the nose, for when it comes to perfumes, today's consumer generally *sees* first and *smells* later! An imposing bottle regally placed amid a countertop display will surely attract more attention than an insignificant one. The factice, or display bottle, is akin to a theater billboard or poster that beckons potential ticket-buyers with its larger-than-life stars and bold colors.

The public is bombarded with a seemingly never-ending parade of new fragrances, making competition understandably keen. How a product is marketed—from advertising to in-store presentation—and the overall packaging is just as important as the scent itself. Both bottle and packaging must be designed and merchandised to create instant attraction. If the first glimpse fails to attract the passersby, the scent it touts may forever remain unknown. As potential buyers scurry through a maze of perfume displays in their favorite department store, the factice occupies the place of honor in this bid for dollars. Standing proud and tall, it is a giant replica of the smaller bottles perfume companies hope browsers will find irresistible.

Understandably, in such a competitive environment, the launching of a new fragrance is an expensive, and highly risky, venture. For example, Dior's *Dune* went "over the top" at twenty million dollars; the launch of Guerlain's *Samsara* cost a reputed fifteen million. Faced with figures of this magnitude, the value of presentation and effective merchandising becomes readily apparent.

In this regard, Elizabeth Taylor's *White Diamonds* has already achieved classic status. The container, designed to replicate the beauty of fine costume jewelry, is a breathtaking example of the heights that can be achieved when bottle designers, scent creators, and advertising and merchandising experts combine their efforts. Susan Wacker, Senior Design Director for Elizabeth Arden, is responsible for its glorious design, which was converted to comprehensive models by Utley's, Inc. With a 40 oz. capacity, the factice is an eye-catching "show-stopper" that commands the same awestruck attention as the star who inspired it.

With its "bigger than life" image, the factice has become a sought-after collectible for many fragrance bottle aficionados. Some include them as adjuncts to their regular bottle collections, some prefer to concentrate on only the factice, and still others simply covet a few bottles for home displays—where they add a dynamic impact to shelves and tub surrounds in the bath, as well as vitrines and wall units elsewhere. No matter for what purpose they are collected or displayed, factice are a feast for the eyes. They are destined to bring much pleasure, whether viewed for a moment or two on a department store counter or as a permanent fixture in one's personal collection.

On the following pages is a representative display of factice, both past and present. They were chosen to portray the beauty and commanding presence of all.

This bottle for *Fleur de Feu* by Guerlain is in a design that also houses other Guerlain fragrances. *Fleur de Feu* was introduced in 1948. 11.5" x 8"

A bottle of massive proportions reminiscent of the medieval, Guerlain's *Mitsouko*. 13.25" x 7.25". The same style flacon was used for other Guerlain fragrances, including *L'Heure Bleue,* its 4" bottle shown here with its "Old World" box. *Mitsouko* was introduced in 1919. *L'Heure Bleue,* introduced in 1912, was designed by Raymond Guerlain, with bottle by Baccarat.

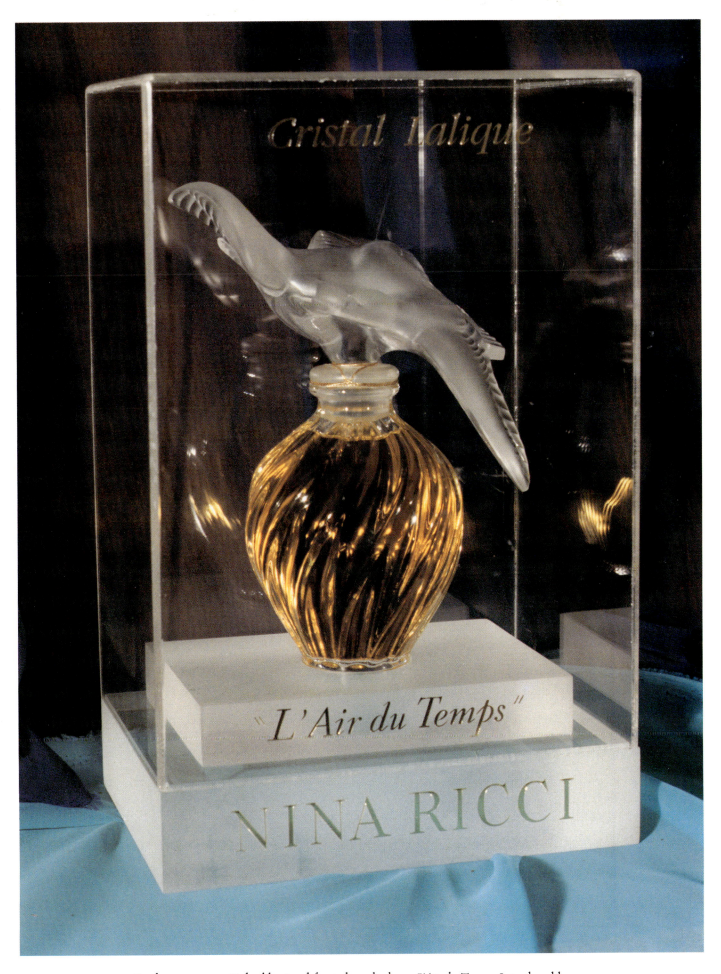

On facing page: a 3" double-tiered frosted acrylic base, *L'Air du Temps*. Introduced by Nina Ricci in 1948 and designed by Marc Lalique, it rises 12". A classic of monumental proportions, the frosted bird has a 13" wingspan. The smaller bottle is 3.5" x 2". The display piece above has an 8" tall bottle, with a wingspan of 7.5". It is protected by a 12" case, and stands on an identical, but smaller, acrylic base.

Most likely a display factice, this crystal beauty touted *Amber* for Charbert during the 1930s-1940s. 7" x 5.25"

Pure elegance . . . *Toujours Moi*, introduced by Corday in 1923. "The bottle, which was designed by René Lalique, is in a shape that suggests a flower oozing with beads of nectar. . . . *Toujours Moi* was used for many years in Parisienne cathedrals as an incense prior to Corday being persuaded to market it as a perfume."[1] With the fragrance now distributed by Max Factor, who bought the company in the early 1960s, it is the only remaining Corday perfume available today. 8.5" factice and 3.5" companion bottle. Made in France.

With white cap of the same design, a pressed glass factice for Roger & Gallet's *Marque Noire*. Introduced in 1891. 9.5" x 5"

Jean d'Albret's gold-entwined *Ecusson*. Introduced in the 1950s. 7.25"

With an elliptical design featuring decorative bands on each side and a striped bottle-green cap, this 9.5" factice was designed for an unidentified Carven fragrance; however, its color and design would suggest that it was for 1957's *Vetiver*.

On stage . . . the curtain rises on Jean d'Albret's *Casque*.
Introduced in the 1950s. 9"

In deep amber-green with a flat stopper, Balmain's *Jolie Madame* factice is 12" high. Introduced in 1953.

With an enormous turban-style stopper, this 10.75" x 7.0" French-made factice is for *Fleur de Monde* by Fabergé, a fragrance produced, bottled, and sealed in France. Introduced in the early 1960s, it was available in the United States in limited quantities for a very short period. A rare and beautiful acquisition, the factice was purchased in Paris and brought to the U.S. shortly after the fragrance was launched. The bottle is by Pochet et du Courval (with HP mark), a glassmaking operation founded in 1623 that continues to produce bottles for prestigious perfume houses.

From the 1930s, this factice promoted an unidentified scent by Carlyle. The 10" x 7.5" bottle, in a fan-shaped, pleated design, has a frosted woodland scene and towering Deco stopper.

Deco delight . . . For counter displays, two Lanvin perfume bottles and a 7.5" jet black glass factice, with complementary black and glass display tray. All feature the now-familiar gold figural emblem of Jeanne Lanvin and her daughter, which was created by Paul Iribe. The bottle was designed by Armand Rateu in 1927 for *Arpege* and later used for *My Sin*.

Bleu De Chine by Marc de la Morandière Parfums, Paris. 9" x 9.5"

Designed to accommodate inside lighting, this 12" high, 8" diameter counter display was for Richard Hudnut's DuBarry line.

Dynamic! *Cabotine* by Gres. The beauty of this 8.5" x 7.5" factice with its frosted green flowers needs no further description. Made in France.

With modernistic grey and gold stopper, *Sybaris* is dynamic in its sleek simplicity. 10" x 8".

This clear crystal beauty serves as a reflecting pool for the floral backdrop of this very feminine *Ruffles* factice. By Oscar de la Renta. Pochet et du Courval "HP" marking. 10" x 9.25"

In a masculine but graceful design, Italian designer Valentino's *Vendetta Pour Homme*. Bottle marked "Made in Italy." Fragrance developed as part of collaboration between Valentino and the Elizabeth Arden Company. 11" x 11.5".

Tresor by Lancome. With a black-rimmed stopper and matching base, an unusual 7.5" x 6.5" design that rises in graduated layers. Made in France.

A lithe, etched and frosted swan graces this 10" factice for *Vanderbilt* by Gloria Vanderbilt.

Weil de Weil in a giant 12.5" height, dramatically topped with a triangular tortoise stopper.

In a timeless, Deco style, this hefty French-made factice is of Jean Patou's *1000*. 6.5" x 6.75".

Crepe De Chine by F. Millot. A dynamic factice with magnificent three-tiered, scalloped stopper featuring an etched and frosted monogram. Made in France. 7.25" x 7.75". A French parfumery since 1839, F. Millot introduced *Crepe de Chine* at the 1900 Paris Exhibition, in a bottle designed by Hector Guimard. The fragrance later became the first to be introduced by the House of Millot in the United States.

Shades of the 1940s... Evyan's *White Shoulders*, introduced in 1943. The matching powder box is of pale pink composition. Note torso figural on bottle and embossed design on box. 11"

With a "Daliesque" design of an illusive female form, *Forever Amber* by Katheryn, Inc., Chicago. Introduced in 1945, its name was undoubtedly derived from the best-selling book and the subsequent movie. This was but one of many popular scents introduced by Katheryn, Inc. (Kay Daumit) during the 1940s. 15".

Imprévu by Coty, introduced in the 1960s. 9.5"

Beautifully faceted, Yves Saint Laurent's factice for *Paris*, introduced in 1983. The fragrance has a Damascenia-rose floral bouquet; the bottle was designed by Alain de Mourgues. 7" x 6"

Although smaller than most, this display bottle is for *Flora Danica*, a fragrance introduced in 1982 and available until 1987. Cut at the bottom to sit on an angle, its concept is unusual in another respect, for the colorful enameled floral design on the back was intended to be viewed through the fragrance. Distributed by Swank, Inc., the bottle is marked "With permission from the Royal Copenhagen Porcelain Manufactory Ltd., Copenhagen, producers of the Flora Danica dinner services since 1796." The 2 oz. bottle is 3.25" x 3" with a heavy crystal stopper.

From Milan, in a deeply faceted design with heavy frosted stopper, this *Mila Schön* factice is 10" high.

A riot of color . . . this veritable garden of enameled flowers covers an enormous 13" x 8" factice of Laura Ashley's *No. 1*. A 4.75" display bottle of more modest size stands proudly by its side. Bottles by Pochet et du Courval.

A gold and enameled 9" leopard languishes on top of this dynamic, ovoid-shaped factice for *Gayle Hayman*. 10" x 7".

Wide and sleek . . . a modernistic design for *Fendi*. 11". Circa 1980s, the fragrance was produced as part of a joint venture with the Elizabeth Arden Company.

Like a glistening mirage in the desert, Christian Dior's *Dune* from 1990. 11" x 8".

With matching mini, this frosted beauty heralds Estee Lauder's *Private Collection*. 10.5".

Tower of Power... Fred Hayman's *273* rises like a crystal obelisk to a height of 12.25".

Elizabeth Taylor's Passion. Her first signature fragrance, it is appropriately fashioned in regal purple, with a diamond-accented center. The modernistically styled, fan-shaped factice is 12" x 8.5".

When the calla lilies are in bloom . . . *Chloé* by Karl Lagerfeld. Whether topping the 9.5" factice, the 3" standard-sized bottle, or the 2" mini, the frosted lily stopper is effective. Containing 178 ingredients, *Chloé* was the first fragrance resulting from Lagerfeld's joint venture with the Elizabeth Arden Company. The bottle was designed by Joe Messina.

Of crackled, frosted glass, this hefty 10.25" factice with Deco-style chrome stopper is *1881* by Nino Cerruti, whose name is boldly lettered in black on each side. This bottle is Italian, and is marked "Nell'Ambriente Dope L'Uso." A renowned name in couture, the Cerruti family firm supplied wool fabrics to the major design houses. The fragrance was named for the street address of designer Nino Cerruti's studio on the Rue Royale in Paris.

Rising 13.5" high, the dynamic color combination of dark blue with crystal-faceted emerald stopper and fuschia ribbon makes this *Ungaro* ribbed bottle with its swirling design very special indeed. The mini provides a startling contrast.

Tasseled and bejeweled. A perfect melding of bottle design with its celebrity name . . . here, three sizes of *Uninhibited* by Cher—a 12" factice, 5.5" retail size, and mini with box.

Sheer beauty that takes bottle design to new heights, J. C. Brousseau's *Ombre Rose*, introduced in 1982. On opposite page, the 11.5" x 8.5" factice, shown with 4.25" retail size, has an intricate pattern of frosted floral designs in high relief. The factice in matte black finish is complemented by the matching heavy-based powder jar. Designed by J. C. Brousseau, the bottles were made in France.

With a giant, undulating, gold stopper, a floral embossed 12" factice for *Oscar de la Renta*.

Celestial delight! A miniature orbits a 9" factice of Karl Lagerfeld's *Sun Moon Stars*, featuring the sun on one side, a crescent moon on the other, and stars all around. With matte gold stopper, this powerful design captures the romance and mystery of the heavenly bodies. To quote Karl Lagerfeld, "The sun, moon and stars have kept the mystery our world has lost . . . here is the unlimited space of sky . . . of dreams, of fantasy." Produced as part of joint venture with Elizabeth Arden Company.

The "giant" of them all! Topped with a swirling design like holiday "ribbon candy," *Romeo Gigli* stands 15" tall on its enormous base.

Of current vintage and with regal color accents of fuschia and royal blue, *Cassini* by couturier Oleg Cassini. Bottle by Pochet et du Courval. 9.5" x 6.5"

In deeply-grooved, blocked design with marbleized blue top, *KL Homme* by Karl Lagerfeld, made in joint venture with Elizabeth Arden Company. Bottle designed by Lagerfeld; produced in France by Pochet et du Courval. 8.5" x 7".

Encased in an ingenious swinging holder, midnight blue and chrome accentuate this masculine deco design for *Monogram* by Ralph Lauren. Note initialed frosted stand and matching mini. 12.5" x 10" overall.

From the Paris house of Maxim, monogrammed 10.5" *Maxim Pour Homme* factice. Made in France and introduced in 1985.

Labeled with the Hermes crest, these display bottles for *Hermes Eau de Cologne* are especially notable for their rich coloration, boldly accented with elegantly understated black stoppers; the teal-green glass reflects the green chypre note and the woody, fruity undertones of the fragrance. The largest bottle measures 10", the smaller, 6.5". Marked "Hermes Paris . . . Made in France." Introduced in 1979.

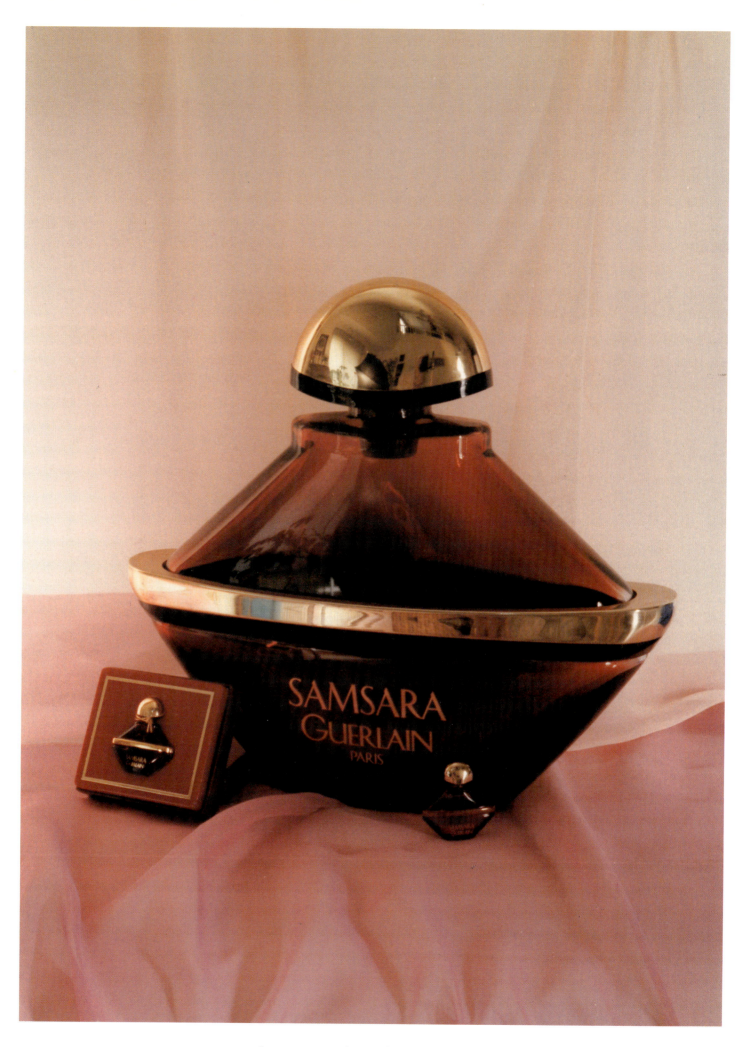

Luscious ruby . . . *Samsara* by Guerlain. 7.75" x 11"

A towering presence . . . Laura Biagiotti's *Venezia*. 15.5" x 9.5"

Liz Claiborne by Liz Claiborne. 13" overall, the massive blue top is a "show stopper," measuring 4.5" x 4".

Liz Claiborne's *Vivid* has an interesting toggle-style topper of royal blue. 14".

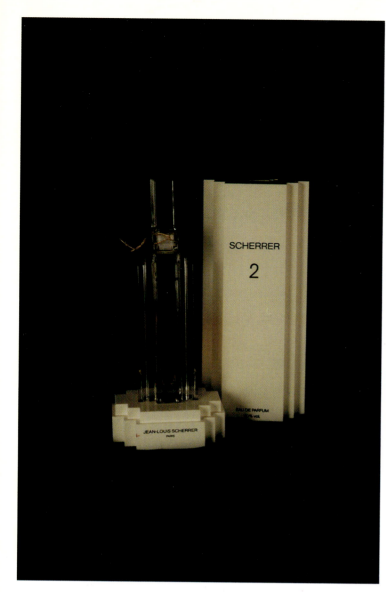

On a complementary, modernistic base, this 7.25" factice is for *Scherrer 2* by Jean-Louis Scherrer, Paris. Introduced in 1986, it brings to mind a towering skyscraper, with its cantilevered style so reminiscent of the Art Deco period. The white composition top is in the same design genre. The fragrance *Scherrer,* with similar ambiance and display base, was designed by Serge Mansau and introduced in 1979. Marked "SGD" (Saint Gobain Desjonquère).

Rising 12" high, this gold-trimmed bottle for *Raffinee* by Houbigant is offset by a deeply-faceted crystal stopper. Launched in 1982, the fragrance of spicy, flowered amber contains over two hundred different products, including many that are considered secret to its formula. The bottle was designed by Alain de Mourgues.

Blushing beauty by the fashion maven . . . a monogrammed *Carolina Herrera*. 12" x 7.5"

Display bottle for *Dioressence* by Christian Dior in a sleek, modernistic design. Introduced in 1979. 5.25"

This factice for French actor Alain Delon's *Le temps d'aimer* is small but mighty . . . a simple design that speaks volumes. 3.75" x 3.0"

Although of lightweight composition, *Opium* by Yves Saint Laurent still "packs a whallop." Crystal-domed, it achieves extra impact with an enormous gold-accented black tassel. Launched in 1977, *Opium* is a spicy floral scent with oriental notes. Bottle designed by Pierre Dinand. 10" x 9.5"

Resembling architectural Art Deco glass blocks, a modernistic factice for Alfred Sung's *Sung*. 10.5" x 7.25".

Like a stately Roman column, *Roma* by Laura Biagiotti. 11.5".

This magnificent factice for *Le Parfum Lalique* stands 10" tall, 7.5" wide, and 1.75" deep. Numbered and marked "Lalique - France."

Dior's *Poison* in the largest of its factice, 13" x 9.5", with giant glass stopper.

This masterpiece of design for *Jean Paul Gaultier* looks like a svelte figure from the workroom of a Parisian fashion house. Made in France. 11.5".

One is magnificent . . . two are a double delight! Rising 10.75", Elizabeth Taylor's *White Diamonds*.

FOOTNOTES

Glassmaking
1 *American Bottles*, 31
2 *Illustrated Guide to American Glass*, 2
3 *Henry Wm. Stiegel*, 193
4 *English Bottles and Decanters*, 7
5 Perfume Bottle Quarterly, Summer 1994
6 *American Bottles*, 28
7 ibid, 28
8 *English Bottles and Decanters*, 14
9 ibid, 78
10 ibid, 79
11 *American Bottles*, 12
12 *Henry Wm. Stiegel*, 197
13 *World of Henry William Stiegel, The*, 6
14 *Illustrated Guide to American Glass*, 52
15 *Henry Wm. Stiegel*, 186
16 ibid, 55
17 200th Anniversary, Zion Evangelical Lutheran Church, 15
18 *American Bottles*, 21
19 *Illustrated Guide to American Glass*, 25
20 ibid, 27
21 ibid, 41
22 *American Bottles*, 126

Historical Perfumeries
1 *Perfume and Pomanders*, 34
2 "Chamerolles, Chateau of Perfumes" brochure
3 ibid
4 ibid
5 ibid
6 "Secret Addresses," *Elle*, May 1995, 182
7 *The Secret Charm of a Perfumed House*, 39
8 ibid, 41
9 ibid, 53
10 ibid, 65
11 ibid, 70
12 ibid, 76
13 ibid, 82
14 ibid, 84
15 ibid, 89
16 ibid, 105
17 ibid, 114
18 ibid, 124

Masterpieces in Modern Glass
1 *Lalique Perfume Bottles*, preface
2 *Lalique Glass*, 16
3 ibid, 17
4 *Perfume and Pomanders*, 75
5 *Lalique Glass*, 10
6 ibid, 61
7 *Old Glass, European and American*, 104

Commercial Flacons
1 *Perfume and Pomanders*, 74
2 *Commercial Fragrance Bottles*, 13

Solid Scents
1 *Perfume and Pomanders*, 17
2 ibid, 27

Factice
1 Mini-Scents Newsletter, Summer 1995

BIBLIOGRAPHY

Adler Picard Tajan catalog, Commissaires-Priseurs Associés; Collection Maria Felix; Paris, France. June 1990.

Ball, Joanne Dubbs and Dorothy Hehl Torem. *Commercial Fragrance Bottles*. Atglen, PA: Schiffer Publishing Ltd., 1993.

Blue, Wendy Hamilton and Dorothy Torem. "Publicity in Hand, a Brief History of Folding Advertising Fans," *Ladies Gallery*. Bay Village, OH: Bay House Publishing, February/March 1995.

Christie's and The Lalique Society of America Exhibition Catalog, 1993.

Churchfield, Melinda. "The History of the Golliwog," *Mini-Scents Newsletter*, Summer 1995.

Colard, Grégoire, translated from the French by Mary Recknell. *The Secret Charm of a Perfumed House*. Paris: J. C. Lattès, 1984.

Davis, Derek C. *English Bottles and Decanters*. New York: The World Publishing Company, 1972.

Dawes, Nicholas M. *Lalique Glass*. New York: Crown Publishers, Inc., 1986.

Drake, Laurie. "Smelling Like a Rose . . . or a Gardenia," *Los Angeles Times*. Los Angeles, CA, July 13, 1995.

Gaborit, Jean-Yves. *Perfumes, The Essences and Their Bottles*. New York: Rizzoli, 1985.

Gavenas, Mary Lisa. "Secret Addresses," *Elle*, May 1995.

Heiges, George L. *Henry Wm. Stiegel*. Published by George L. Heiges: Manheim, PA, 1948.

Kendig, John D. *The Worlds of Henry William Stiegel*. Manheim, PA, 1977.

Ketchum, William C., Jr. *A Treasury of American Bottles*. Indianapolis, IN and New York: Bobbs-Merrill, 1975.

Launert, Edmund. *Perfume and Pomanders*. North Yorkshire, England: Potterton Books, 1987.

The Loiret Department Conseil General. "Chamerolles, Chateau of Perfumes" brochure. France.

Monsen and Baer Perfume Bottle Auction Catalogs. Monsen and Baer, Vienna, VA, 1991 and 1992.

Moore, N. Hudson. *Old Glass, European and American*. New York: Frederick A. Stokes Company, 1924.

North, Jacquelyne Y. Jones. *Commercial Perfume Bottles*. West Chester, PA: Schiffer Publishing Ltd., 1987.

North, Jacquelyne Y. Jones. *Perfume, Cologne and Scent Bottles*. West Chester, PA: Schiffer Publishing Ltd., 1986.

Papert, Emma. *The Illustrated Guide to American Glass*. New York: Hawthorn Books, Inc., 1972.

Perfume and Scent Bottle News. Rockford, Illinois.

Perfume and Scent Bottle Quarterly. Galena, Ohio.

Stage. Ince Publishing Co., Inc., New York. December 1940.

"200th Anniversary, Zion Evangelical Lutheran Church." Manheim, Pennsylvania. 1972.

Utt, Mary Lou and Glenn, with Patricia Boyer. *Lalique Perfume Bottles*. New York: Crown Publishers, Inc., 1990.

Vogue. Condé Nast Publications, Inc., New York. April 1939.

White, Palmer. *Elsa Schiaparelli*. New York: Rizzoli, 1986.

VALUE GUIDE

These values represent a general assessment of current market conditions. Be aware that many factors influence variations in price, including geographical location, condition of the bottle, and the trends of the fragrance bottle collecting world. These evaluations are meant to serve merely as guidelines; collectors must also rely on their own good judgment and preferences. Except for factice, and with certain other exceptions, bottles for more recently introduced fragrances will not be valued.

The first column indicates the page number on which a bottle can be found. The second column indicates the bottle's position on that page-Right, Left, Bottom, etc. The last column provides the value range, in U.S. dollars.

Key:

* = Due to market fluctuations, values for Lalique bottles will not be included in this guide; it is recommended that current valuations be obtained from an accredited expert or dealer.

** = Values of these bottles are in the "1000 up" range, with many considerably higher. All can be further influenced by condition, rarity, and completeness of presentation.

N/A = Not available; many are museum pieces and not available for valuation.

Page	Position	Value
3		**
4		500-1000
5		500 up
6		500-1000
11	TR	N/A
	BL	500-800
	BR	150-250
12	l. to r.	1000-1500
		800-1200
		500-800
		500-800
14		N/A
15		N/A
19		N/A
21	TR	175-250
	B-l. to r.	300-500
		300-500
		300-500
		200-300
22	T-l. to r.	250-400
		250-400
		250-400
		200-300
	CR	75-125
	BL	45-60
30	BL	**
31	TR	100 up
	B	175-250 w/box
32	TL	250-500
	TR	175-250
	BL	100 up
34	T	current
	B	225-350
36	TL	100 up
	BR	150 up
27		150 up/set of 3
28	TL	current
	BL	100 up
	BR	50 up
29	T	500-750
	B	145-175
40		current
41		current
42		all current
43	T	**
	B	current
44		**/each
45-52		*
52	B	100-150
53	TR	500 up
	BL	**
	BR	250-350
54	TL	**
	TR	500-1000
	BL	**
55		200 up/pr.
56	L	300 up
	R	125-175

Page	Position	Value
57	clockwise	800 up
		125-175
		20-30
		300 up
58	T	current
	B	75-125
59	T	800 up
60	T	**
	B	**
61		Rare, N/A
62	T	500 up
	B	**/set
63	TL	200 up
	CR	200 up
	BL	225 up
64	T	800 up
	B	400 up
65	T	250-350/each
	B	800 up
66	L	200 up/each
	R	350 up
67		1200 up
68		300-500
69	TL	500-1000
	C	500-1000
	B	500 up
70	TL	400-500
	TR	350-450
	BL	400-500
	BR	400-500
71	TL	**
	C	1800 up
	B	500 up
72		400-500
73		350 up
74	T	250-400
	B	350-550
75	T	350-500
	B	250-300
76	TR	250-300
	CL	400-550
	BR	400-500
77	TR	250-400
	BL	500-1000
78	T	200 up
	B	250-350
79	T	175-225
	CL	225-275
	BR	225-275
80		250-350
81		200-350
82	TR	400-500
	L	350-450
	BR	300-450
83	BL	225-275
	BR	200-250
84	L	250-300
	R	300-400/set

251

Page	Pos	Price
85		800 up/pr.
86	L	800 up
	TR	300-500
	BR	150-200
87	T	50-75
	B	300 up
88		400 up
89	T	200-300
	CR	85-125/pr.
	BL	250-325
90	TL	35-50/ea.
	TR	100-150
	BL	100 up/ea.
	BR	current
91		**
92	TL	1000 up
	TR	250 up
	BR	150 up
93		85-125
94		500-1000
95		250-500
96	T	250-500
	BL	125 up
	BR	175 up
97	TL	100 up
	CR	**
	BL	150-250
100		65-85
101		500 up
102	B	**
103		150 up
104		*
108	TL	**
	R	100-150
	BL	**
109	TL	500-1000
	B	250-500
110		500-1000
111	B	250-500
112	T	**
	B	**
113		150 up
114	L	500-1000
115	TL	1200 up
	BL	200-300
116		400-600
117	T	150-250
	B	300-450
118	L	*
119	T	current
	BL	125-175
	BR	150-275
125	TL	135-200
	B	300 up
126	T-l.	50-75
	-r.	100 up
	B	20-50/ea.
127	T	**
	BL	250-500
	BR	175-250
129		200-300
130	T-l.	500-700
	T-r.	200-300
	CR	125-175
	BL	100 up
131	T	125-175
	B	150-200
132	T	175-250
	B	150-225/set

Page	Pos	Price
133	TL	125-175
	TR	45-65
	B	75-100/pr.
134		800 up
136	TL	85-125
	BR	150-250
137	TL	85-125
	CR	175-300
	B	275 up
138	TL	500 up
	TR	275 up
	B	100-125
139	front center	200-300
	all others under $100/ea.	
140	TL	250 up
	TR	175-250
	B	175-225/4 pc.set
142		800 up
143	TL	250-500
	TR	250 up
	BR	125-150
144		250-500
145	T	175-250
	B-l.	300 up
	-r.	150-200
146	T	125-200
	B	100-150
147	TL	250 up
	CR	175-250
148	T	300-500
	BL	50-100
	BR	*
152	TL	500-1000 w/box
	TR	current
	B	*
153		300 up
154		current
155	TR	current
	B	175-250
156	TL	current
	TR	35-50/ea.
	BR	75-125
157	TL	30-45
	TR	current
	B	current
158	TL	current
	TR	current
	BL	45-65
	BR	current
159	TL	*
	TR	150-175
	BL	75-125
	BR	150-175
160	TL	150-175
	TR	150-175
	BL	150-175
	BR	150-175
161	TL	175-250
	TR	250-300
	B	200-250
162	TR	50-75
	BL	100-175
163	TL	50-75
	CR	25 up/ea.
	BL	35-50/ea.
164	T	275 up
	B	25-45
165	T	150 up
	B	250 up

Page	Pos	Price
166	T l. to r.	20-30
		35-55
		40-60
	B	150 up
167	TL	150 up
	TR	100 up
	BL	250-500
	BR	100 up
168	TL	65-100 w/box
	TR	100 up w/box
	BL	100 up
	BR	125 up
169	T	100 up w/box
	C	100 up w/box
	B	100 up w/box
170	T	75-100/set
	C	100 up/ea.
	B	100 up
171	TL	100 up
	TR	50 up
	B	50-65
172		125 up
173	TL	250 up
	CR	75-100
	BL	100 up
174	TL	250-350
	TR	100 up
	BR-l.	30-40
	-r.	125-175/set
175	TL	65-85
	CR	25-35/ea.
	BL	50-75
176	TL	45-65
	TR	25-35
	BR	35-50
177	TL	current
	CR	current
	BL	current
178	TL	35-50
	TR	current
	BR	all current
179	TL	current
	TR-l.	20-30
	-r.	30-45
	BL	current
	BR	45-60
180	TL	300/set
	BL	75-100
	BR	75-100
181	TL	60-75
	TR	20-35/ea.
	CL	50-75 ea.
	CR, l. to r.	100-125
		200-300
		50-65
	BL	50-75 ea.
	BR	55-85 ea.
182	T	75-125
	B, l.	100 up
	B, r.	65-85
183-8	All fans	100 up
190		300-450
191	rear	900 up
	front	125-175 w/box
192		1500 up
193		1500 up
194		250-300
195	rear	700 up
	front	225-325 w/box

Page	Pos	Price
196		175-250
197		200-275
198		175-300
199		200-300
200		200-300
201		1200 up
202		500 up
203	T, rear	250-300
	T, front	150-200/set
	B	275-375
204		175-250
205	TL	350-500
	BR	175-250
206		275-375
207		200-300
208	TL	250-350
	BR	200-300
209		400-500
210		400-600
211		400-600
212		200-275/bottle
		100-150/powder
213		350-500
214		300-400
215	T	275-375
	B	145-175
216		300-400
217	rear	600-800
	front	125-175
218	T	700 up
	B	275-375
219		275-375
220		250-350
221		900 up
222		500-700
223		300-450
224	TL	350-500
	BR	600-800
225	rear	600-800
	front l.	85-135
	front r.	45-65
226		400-500
		125-150/powder
227	r.	350-500
	f.	125-150
228	TL	225-350
	BR	500 up
229		800 up
230	TL	250-350
	BR	200-350
231		700 up
232		125-175
233	rear	275-350
	front	175-250
234		350-500
235		350-450
236		275-350
237		300-375
238	TL	175-200
	BR	375-500
239		350-500
240		150-200
241		100-150
242		350-450
243		350-500
244		300-400
245		*
246		450-650
247		600 up
248		1000 up/ea.

General Index

Advertising Age, 42
Amelung, John Frederick, 17, 18, 20, 21
American Flint Glass Manufactory, 14
American Revolution, 18
Andrew Jergens Co., 108
Apollo, 79, 83
Arden, Elizabeth, 9, 38, 39, 40, 41, 42, 54, 105, 141, 166, 189, 207, 218, 223, 228, 230
Arly, 117
Art, Gout, Beaute, 49, 114
Arys, 50
Ashley, Laura, 217
Avon, 176, 181
Ayers, Harriet Hubbard, 165, 167

B.D. Baldwin Co., 113
Babani, 87, 104, 105
Baccarat, 26, 29, 37, 38, 53, 54, 127, 129, 133, 191
Balmain, 200
Bataille, Maurice, 34, 36
Bergaud, Jean, 34, 37
Bertelli, 144
Bertrand, Henry, 37, 38
Biagiotti, Laura, 235, 244
Blue Waltz, 118
Bohemian glass, 68, 89
Borghese, Princess Marcella, 180
Boston and Sandwich Works, 21
Boucher, Claude, 47
Bourjois, 20, 120, 140, 141, 175
Bouton, 99, 175
Bristol glass, 86
Brossard family, 24
Brousseau, J. C., 226

Cacharel, 152
Calixte, 124
Captiband Perfumes Ltd., 100
Cardinal de Richelieu, 25
Carlyle, 202
Carnegie, Hattie, 142, 143
Caron, Anna-Marie, 31, 33
Caron, 30, 31, 32, 33, 34, 35, 36, 37, 38, 50, 120, 141, 179, 163
Carven, 121, 157, 198
Cassini, Oleg, 230
Castex, Francòis, 37
Century, 98
Cerbelaud, R., 109
Cerruti, Nino, 224
Chamerolles, 24, 26
Chanel, 26, 121, 126
Charbert, 141, 194
Charles X, 25
Charles of the Ritz, 47, 109, 141
Chelsea, 9
Cher, 176, 225
Cherigan, 119
Chess, Mary, 111, 119
Ciro, 168
Claiborne, Liz, 236, 237
Coetlogon family, 24
Columbian Air Ship, 92
Combs-la-Ville, 47
Conde-Nast, 37
Continental Army, 18
Corday, 50, 138, 141, 151, 165, 195
Coryse, 50
Coty, Francois, 47, 91
Coty, 20, 26, 50, 99, 122, 131, 137, 141, 166, 168, 214
Coventry Glass Factory Co., 20
Créey en Valois, 9
Crown Perfumery Co., 27, 28, 29

d'Albret, Jean, 197, 199
d'Artiques, Monsieur, 53
D'aumont, Madame La Marechale, 29
D'Orsay, 50, 51, 97, 122, 137, 147, 148, 170
Dali, Salvador, 127, 176
Daltroff, Ernest, 30, 31, 32, 33, 34, 38
Dana, 124, 180
Danner, George, 14, 15
Daum, 26
Daumit, Kay, 213
de Faros, 141
de la Renta, Oscar, 157, 178, 206, 228
de Molinas, 110
de Parys, Jean, 50, 51
Dépinoix, 97
DeCameron, Inc., 105
Delon, Alain, 241
Deltah, 163
DeMeyer, Baron, 105
DeRaymond, 134
Derby, 87
Desgrippes, Joel, 38
Desjonquère, Saint Gobain, 55, 238
Desprez, Jean, 10, 57, 152, 179
DeVilbiss, 52
DeVilbiss, Dr. Alan, 52
DeVilbiss, Dr. Thomas, 52
DeVilbiss Imperial Line, 53
Dinand, Pierre, 38, 57, 242
Dior, Christian, 4, 26, 132, 189, 219, 240, 246
Dralle-Hamburg, 60
Du Lac family, 24
DuBarry, 204
Duncan, Isadora, 110
Dune, Pierre, 110

Edward IV, 87
Edward VII, 27
Eli Lilly & Co., 39
Elizabeth Furnace, 13
Elkann, Jean-Paul, 37
Ellenville Glass Works, 20
Enlightenment, The, 26
Evyan, 212

Faberge, 39, 133, 155, 171, 180, 201
Factor, Max, 181, 182, 195
Fantine, 97
Fellers, 86
Festival of the Red Rose, 16
Fifi Awards, 42
Fini, Leonor, 129
Fioret, 50
Florenza, 181
Fontanis, 91
Forvil, 50
Fragonard, 50, 57, 174
Fragrance Foundation, 42
Franck, Marcel, 90
Francois I, 24
Franklin, Benjamin, 18
Frontincennes, 7
Fulton, Robert, 14
Furstenberg, 9

Gaillard, Lucien, 55
Galerie Lafayette, 188
Gallatin Company, 17, 18
Gallatin, Albert, 17, 18
Gallé, 44
Gibson, Barry, 29
Gigli, Romeo, 158, 229
Givenchy, 56, 163
Glamour, 42
Goebel of Germany, 87
Goya, 171
Gray, Dorothy, 141, 168
Gres, 179, 205
Griffe, Jacques, 143
Gualtier, Jean Paul, 247
Guerlain, 20, 26, 37, 53, 123, 133, 145, 148, 177, 189, 190
Guerlain, Raymond, 191
Guerycolas, D., 129
Guimard, Hector, 211

Harmony Glass Works, 20
Harper's Bazaar, 105
Hayman, Fred, 221
Hayman, Gayle, 218
Helleu, Jacques, 126
Hermes, 101, 233
Herrera, Carolina, 239
Hershey, Milton S., 14
Hershey Museum, 15
Hewes, Robert, 20
Hoffman, Heinrich, 61, 71
Holz, Elizabeth, 13
Houbigant, 50, 53, 98, 123, 141, 238
House of Chloe, 41
Huber, Jacob, 13
Hudnut, Richard, 93, 130, 138, 141, 146, 167, 204
Hummelshein, Walter, 36

Iribe, Paul, 203
Isaacs, Lazarus, 14
Isabey, 50, 112
Isadora, 110, 153, 179

Jefferson, Thomas, 17
Jollivet, 134
Joubert, 118
Jovan, 156
Justin, J. G., 89

Kahann, Monsieur, 30, 31, 33
Katheryn, Inc., 213
King Tut, 7
Klein, Calvin, 157
Knights of the Round Table, 24
Kramer, Balthazer, 17, 18
Krizia, 158

L. T. Piver, 50, 54, 106, 107, 108, 124, 143, 186
la Rose Dorée, 97
La Gazette du Bon Ton, 102, 107
Lacroix, Christian, 178
Ladies Home Journal, The, 16
Lady Grey, 130
Lagerfeld, Karl, 41, 178, 179, 223, 228, 230
Lalique, 152, 159
Lalique, Rene, 6, 26, 45, 46, 47, 48, 49, 50, 51, 52, 55, 118, 152, 245
Lalique, Mark, 50, 148, 193
Lalique, Marie-Claude, 50, 51, 159
Lambert, Guillame, 25
Lambert family, 24
Lancelot the First, 24
Lancome, 26, 47, 115, 121, 174, 178, 208
Lanvin, 26, 50, 87, 121, 203
Lanvin, Jeanne, 203
LaRoche, Guy, 156
Lauder, Estee, 180, 181, 220
Lauren, Ralph, 158, 177, 231
Lee, James, 20
Lefort, Monsieur, 31, 38
Lelong, Lucien, 50, 121, 141, 166, 169
Lengyel, 49, 141
Lentheric, 122, 135, 141, 169
Les Parfums de Rosine, 3, 112
Libbey, Edward, 21
Libbey, William, 21
LiLi, 141
Linus Pauling Institute, 40
Lionceau, 143
Loiret Dept. Conseil Général, 24
Louis XVI, 25
Louis, XII, 24, 25
Lubin, 108, 122
Lynas, 115
Lynette, 136

Magasin Caron, 31
Maine Chance Spa, 39
Manheim Glass Works, 14
Mansau, Serge, 37, 238

Matchabelli, 20, 122, 138, 139, 140, 141, 172
Maublanc, Vicomtesse de, 38
Maugenet, Leon, 164
Maxim, 232
Meissen, 9
Messina, Joe, 223
millifiori, 8
Millot, F., 167, 211
Moiret, 119
Molinard, 50, 132
Molyneaux, 50, 120
Morandière, Mark, 203
Morsetti, Monsieur, 36, 37
Mourgues, Alain de, 215, 238
Mucha, Alphonse, 99
Murano, 26
Museum of American Glass, 19
Myrugia, 125, 146, 164

Napoleon III, 5, 63, 64, 65
Negré, Monsieur, 37
Nell-Ambriente Dope L'Uso, 224
New Breman Glass Works, 17
New England Glass Co., 20, 21, 22
Nicholson, James, 17

opaline, 5, 62, 63, 64, 65, 66, 67, 166
Orlane, 47
Orloff, 137

Palmer, Solon, 168
Palomeras and Pucci Ltd., 187
Paquin, 121
Parfumerie Emilia, 30
Park & Tilford, 175
Parkinson, George Robert, 129
Patou, Jean, 38, 123, 133, 210
Pennsylvania Gazette, 13
Pequette, 141
Peri Khasana, 150
Philadelphia Novelty & Perfume Co., 92
Picasso, Paloma, 156, 177
Piguet, Robert, 123
Pinaud, Ed., 102
Pitkin Glass Co., 20
Pochet Et Du Courval, 38, 55, 56, 57, 58, 118, 158, 201, 206, 217, 230
Poiret, Paul, 3, 26, 112
pressed glass, 22

Queen Victoria, 27

Ramses, 60
Raphael, 123
Rateu, Armand, 203
Renaud, 167
Renoir, 120
Revillon, 131
Revlon, 181
Ricci, Nina, 50, 123, 148, 152, 192, 193
Rigaud, 117
Robins family, 37
Rochambeau, 136
Rochas, Marcel, 55, 122
Roger et Gallet, 26, 45, 50, 94, 96, 147, 196
Ronni Perfumes Inc., 163
Rosenstein, Nettie, 145
Ross, Charlie, 21
Rothschild, Nadine de, 37
Rothschild, Alain de, 37
Royal Copenhagen, 215
Rubenstein, Helena, 141, 170, 181

Saint Gaudens, 111
Saint Laurent, Yves, 215, 242
Saint-Louis, 26
sandwich glass, 21, 22
Saumery family, 24
Scherrer, Jean-Louis, 238
Schiaparelli, 127, 128, 141, 170, 173, 181
Shulton, 141
Sidon, 102
Simpson, Wallis, 27
South Jersey glass, 18, 19
Spa Skincare, 40
Spode, 87
Squibb Pharmaceutical Co., 39
St. Denis, 141
Staffordshire, 9
Stage magazine, 129, 141, 149, 151
Stanger brothers, 18, 21
Stanger, Solomon, 19
Steuben Gold Aurene, 71
Stiegel, Henry William, 12, 13, 14, 15, 16, 17, 18, 19, 20, 21
Studio Rochas, 55
Sung, Alfred, 243
Swank, 215

Tamerlane, 8
Taylor Elizabeth, 41, 179, 189, 222, 248
Thiel, Vicki, 154
Thompson family, 29
Thomson, William Sparks, 27
Tuthmosis III, 7

Ultima II, 155
Ungaro, 224
Unilever Prestige Personal Products, 39
Upton, Florence, 116
Utley's, Inc., 189

Valentino, 42, 206
Van Cleef and Arpels, 58
Vanderbilt, Lucretia, 174
Vanderbilt, Gloria, 208
Vanpouille, Félicie (Madame Bergaud), 31, 32, 33, 34, 36, 37, 38
Venetian glass, 85, 161
Venetian Toilet Preparations, 105
Veolay, 50
Verreries Brosse, 38, 59, 116, 126
Versace, Gianni, 158
Verté, Marcel, 129
Viard, J., 59
Vieux-Rouen, 90
Vigny, 50, 116
Villard, J., 59
Vionnet, 114
Vivelle, 95
Vivi, 103
Vogue, 37, 135
Vougay, 115

Wacker, Susan, 189
Wanamaker, John, 92
War of the Tulips, 26
Weil, Raymond, 124, 209
West, Mae, 129
Wheaton Glass Co., 20, 143
Wheaton, Dr. Theodore, 20
Wheaton, Frank Hayes, 20
Williamstown Glass Works, 19
Wistar, Caspar, 17, 18
Wistarberg Glass House, 18
Worth, 6, 47, 49, 50, 120

Yardley, 141, 169
Ybry, 114

Fragrance Names Index

Abano, 139
Abientôt, 135
Acasciosa, 32
Afghani, 104
Alpona, 30
Amber, 194
Ambre De Nubie, 60
Ambre De Delhi, 104
Ambre de Carthage, 112
Amphitrite, 52
Anticipation, 135
Antilope, 124
Arden Rose, 40
Arden Jasmine, 40
Arpege, 203
Astris, 54
Asuma, 168
Aux Liserous en Verre, 44
Ave Maria, 172

"b", 114
Baccara, 143
Bain Sacre, 35, 38
Bal à Versailles, 57, 152, 179
Balalaika, 166
Bandit, 123
Bellodgia, 31, 31, 35, 141
Ben Hur, 108
Bessor, 132
Black Rose, 171
Black Pearls, 43
Black Lace, 40
Blackout, 41
Blason, 164
Bleu de Chine, 112, 203
Blue Grass, 39, 40
Bohême, 117
Bois des Iles, 125
Bois des Fles, 121
Bond Street, 141
Bouchon Cassie, 46
Bouquet Largillière, 94
Bouton de Rose, 99
Box Office, 40
Bretton Woods, 141
Brise d' Orient, 40

C'est la vie!, 178
Cabotine, 179, 205
Caresse, 174
Carnival, 40
Carolina Herrera, 239
Casaque, 199
Casini, 230
Chamade, 148

Chanel No. 5, 126
Chantecler, 32
Chloé Narcisse, 41
Chloé, 41, 179, 223
Chypre, 105, 130, 163
Ciara, 181
Cigalia, 45
Coco, 126
Coeur Joie, 123
Confetti, 122, 141
Coque d'Or, 53
Corsage, 40
Corylopsis, 97
Country, 170
Crab Apple Blossom, 27, 28
Crepe de Chine, 167, 211
Crown Bouquet, 29
Crown Heliotrope, 29
Crown Jewel, 138
Crown Marechale 29, 90
Crown Matsukita, 29
Cuir de Russie, 124, 125
Cuir Du Canada, 124
Cupid's Breath, 40
Cyclamen, 40, 43, 136

Daimo, 104
Daniel de Fasson, 58
Dans La Nuit, 49
Daybreak, 141
Desire, 175
Desti, 183
Diamonds and Sapphires, 42
Diamonds and Rubies, 42
Diamonds and Emeralds, 41
Diorama, 4
Dioressence, 240
Diorissimo, 132
Directoire, 109
Divertissement, 112
Divine, 122, 137
Doblis, 101
Dress Parade, 168
Duchess of York, 172
Dune, 189, 219

Eau de France, 41
Eau de Caron, 38
Ebbrezza Marina, 144
Ecusson, 197
"1881," 224
Elizabeth Taylor's Passion, 41, 179, 222

Emeraude, 137, 166
Emilie, 174
En Verre E' Maillé, 44
En Avion, 35
Enigma, 108
Enterdit, 56
Envie, 122
Essence Imperiale Russe, 141
Etoile De Napoleon, 95
Evening in Paris, 140, 175
Ever After, 121
Extrait D'Ambre Gris, 105

Faune, 47
Femme, 122
Femme De Paris, 114
Fendi, 41, 218
Fendi Asja, 41
Fendi Uomo, 41
Fetiche, 106
Fiami, 180
Fille d'Eve, 50
First, 58
Flair, 169
Fleur de Monde, 201
Fleur de Rocaille, 33, 38
Fleur de Feu, 190
Fleurs d'Annam, 104
Fleurs d' Amour, 96
Fleurs De Rocaille, 31, 33, 35, 38
Fleurs d'Elle, 145
Fleurs De Pommier, 51
Flora Danica, 215
Flutter, 141
For Her, 40
Forever Amber, 213
"49," 143
Fougeres, 45
Four Muses, The, 50, 51
French Cancan, 35

Gala Nights, 175
Gardenia, 119, 125
Gayle Hayman, 218
Gemey, 146
Gianni Versace, 158
Giardini, 105
Giorgio, 59
Gone with the Wind, 40
Grace, 51
Grande Epoque, 120
Grilou, 143

Hattie Carnegie, 142
Head Over Heels, 155
Hermes Eau de Cologne, 233
High Heels, 175
Hypnotique, 182

I élan d'elizabeth, 40
Imprévu, 214
Imprudence, 47
Indiscret, 121
Infini, 37, 38
Isadora, 110, 153, 179
It's You, 40, 54, 141
Italian Lilac, 40

Jabot, 169
Jacinthe Précieuse, 33
Jasmin De Corée, 105
Jasmine, 48, 51
Jean Paul Gualtier, 247
Jet, 141, 151
Jicky, 133
Jockey Club, 164
Jolie Madame, 200
Jolie Marquis, 110
Joyau, 155
June Geranium, 40
Jungle Flower, 122

Katherine the Great, 172
Kiku, 171
Kismet, 100
KL, 41
Krazy Krizia, 158
Kyphi, 7

L' amour d'elizabeth, 40
L'Aimant, 122
L'air du Temps, 148, 192, 193
L'Ardente Nuit, 138
L'Heure Bleue, 191
L'Infini, 33
L'Interdit, 163
la Jardin d'Elizabeth, 40
la Joie d'Elizabeth, 40
La Nativité, 115
La Perle d'Isabey, 112
Ladies and Gentlemen, 41
Lady, 134
Lady in Black, 41
Lady Luxury, 115
Lagerfeld, 41
Lagerfeld Photo, 41
Larose, 130
Lauren, 158
Lavender Smelling Salts, 27, 28, 29
le amour d'elizabeth, 40
Le Baiser du Faune, 46
le bouquet d'elizabeth, 40
Le Corail Rouge, 46
Le Début Vert, 167
Le De Givenchy, 56
Le Dandy, 148
le etoile d'elizabeth, 40

le êve d'elizabeth, 40
Le Golliwogg, 116
Le Jade, 147
Le Lys d'Isabey, 97
Le Narcisse Noir, 163
Le Nu, 50, 51
Le Pois de Senteur, 167
Le Prestige, 119
Le Roi Soleil, 127
Le Soirée, 138
le temps d'aimer, 241
Le Weekend, 90
Les Parfum Lalique, 48, 50, 159, 245
Les Perles, 48
Les Iscles d'Or, 118
Les Yeux Bleus, 46
Lido, 141
Liglia, 104
LiLi, 141
Lily of the Valley, 163
Liz Claiborne, 236
Lohse Uralt Lavendel, 150
Lou Lou, 152
Lov' Me, 118
Lucretia Vanderbilt, 174
Lumière, 55
Lys, 112

M'Lati, 188
Ma Rue, 40
Ma Griffe, 121, 157
Madhva, 91
Madras De Oriente, 125
Magie Noire, 174
Magnificence, 120
Mais Oui, 141
Marque Noir, 196
Marrakech, 121
Mascarades, 119
Masque Rouge, 184
Maxim Pour Homme, 232
Mazurka, 174
Mémoire Chéie, 39, 41
Meteor, 130
Mila Schöen, 216
Millie Fleurs, 41
Milord, 147, 170
Ming, 104
Ming Toy, 54
Miracle, 135
Miss Jezebel, 40
Mitsouko, 191
Modernis, 32
Molinard De Molinard, 118
Moment Supreme, 133
Mon Boudoir, 98
Mon Amour, 41
Mon Amie Elizabeth, 105
Monogram, 177, 231
Moss Rose, 141

Mountie, 41
Mouson Lavendel, 150
Muguet De Bonheur, 36, 37
Muguet, 99, 135
Murmure, 174
My Sin, 203
My Love, 41, 166

N'aimez que Moi, 33
Nandita, 105
Narcisse Noir, 33, 34
Natouna, 174
Nebula, 102
Nenuphar, 99
Nikki, 137
No. 3, 175
No. 1, 217
Nocturnes, 37, 38, 179
Normandie, 123
Nothing Sacred, 40
Nueva Maja, 146
Nuit de Noel, 34, 35, 36

Obsession, 157
Odalisque, 145
Oh la la, 168
Oillet, 104
Old Spice, 141
Ombre Rose, 226, 227
"1000," 210
Opening Night, 141
Opium, 242
Or et Noir, 32, 36
Oreade, 186
Oscar de la Renta, 228
Osé, 156
Oui Madame, 174

Paloma Picasso, 156, 176
Parfum Sacre, 35, 38
Parfum de La Parisienne, 109
Parfum Impérial, 49
Parfum Pour Brunes, 143
Paris, 149, 215
Pave Elle, 176
Peau Fine, 33
Pierrot, 3
Pink Clover, 165
Pleasant Memories, 103
Plein Ete, 123
Pois de Senteur, 38
Poison, 246
Pour Un Homme, 38
Pravia, 102
Prince's Feather, 40
Princess of Wales, 141
Printanel, 106
Private Collection, 220
Profile, 41

Queen Mary, 92
Quelques Fleur, 53

R.S.V.P., 141
Radiant, 32
Rafinee, 238
Ramses, 102
Rare Orchid, 163
Raverie De Fleurs, 130
Ravissement, 32
Red Door, 40
RendeVous, 174
Repartee, 169
Replique, 123
Requête, 6, 120
Reve de Grasse, 174
Reve Indien, 174
Roma, 244
Romeo Gigli, 158, 229
Rose Précieuse, 33
Rose Gullistan, 104
Roses D'Orsay, 97
Royal Bain De Champagne, 34, 36
Royal Caron, 32
Ruffles, 206
Rumeur, 121

S, 129
Saigon, 104
Salvador Dali, 176
San Adieu, 47
Savoir Faire, 168
Scarabee, 107
Scherrer, 238
Scherrer 2, 238
Sculptura, 156
Shalimar, 145
Shanghai, 135
Shocking, 125, 127, 173
Si, 130
Sirène, 154
Sirenes, 49
Sleeping, 129, 130, 141
Slumber Song, 141
Snuff, 129
Soir de Paris, 120
Sortilege, 163
Souci, 129
Sourire Fleuri, 112
Sous le Gui, 51
Sousouki, 105
Souvenir D'Un Soir, 111
Spellbound, 136
Sphinx, 60
Spring Song, 182
Stradivari, 139
Succès Fou, 170
Sun Moon Stars, 41, 178, 228

Sunflower, 42
Sung, 243
Surprise, 41
Sweet Pea Ambree, 115
Sybaris, 205

Tabac Blond, 35
Tabu, 180
Thousand Flowers, 41
Three Flowers, 130
Tosca, 150
Toujours Moi, 195
Tout Mon Jardin, 93
Town, 170
Transparence, 141
Trésor, 178, 208
True Love, 42
Tuberose d'Elizabeth, 40
Tweed, 135
"273," 221

Ulysse, 124
Un Air Embaume, 117
Ungaro, 178, 223
Uninhibited, 176, 225

Valleé des Rois, 108, 185
Vanderbilt, 208
Velva, 49
Venezia, 235
Vera-Violetta, 96
Verte, 139
Vertige, 141
Vetiver, 198
Violet, 164
Vivid, 237
Voeu de Noel, 120
Vol de Nuit, 123
Volt, 106
Volupté, 157, 178
Voyage a Paris, 165

Weil de Weil, 209
White Shoulders, 212
White Diamonds, 41, 42, 179, 189, 248
White Lilac, 141
Wild Plum Blossom, 113
Wind Song, 139
Winged Victory, 41
With Pleasure, 34

Yasmak, 104
Younger Set, 41
Yram, 119

Zombie, 141
Zut, 129